T0149885

Almost the Only BRIDGE BOOK You Will Ever Need

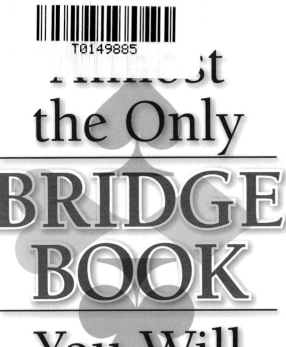

• VOLUME ONE •

RANDY BARON

BARON BARCLAY
BRIDGE SUPPLY

Practice. Play. Teach.

Copyright 2018 Baron Barclay Bridge Supplies

All rights reserved. No part of this book may be reproduced
in any form without the permission of the publisher.

PUBLISHED BY:

Baron Barclay Bridge Supplies
3600 Chamberlain Lane, Suite 206
Louisville, KY 40241
U.S. & Canada 1-800-274-2221
Worldwide 502-426-0410
Fax 502-426-2044
www.baronbarclay.com

ISBN: 978-1-944201-15-9

Cover design by Mary Maier
Text design and composition by John Reinhardt Book Design

Printed in the United States of America

To Mary, Devyn, Richie, Jackson, Dustin & Sarah
who make Louisville and the world joyful

Contents

SECTION ONE

Having Fun and Useful Habits

SECTION TWO

Your System, Conventions, and Strategy

Acknowledgments

To Lee Bukstel, Verna Goldberg, Ralph Letizia,
Bill McAvinue, Jim Morguelan & Norman Morris
for their help in organizing and improving my writing

To Brent Manley for his brilliant editing,
making it appear that I am somewhat literate

To Frank Stewart for his frequent invaluable advice
and impeccable writing

To my friends who agreed to include an essay
which improved the quality of the book greatly

To John Reinhardt, the world's best book designer

To Jimmy Maier for being an extraordinary partner
for over 20 years and who has never spoken a single
unkind word to me (even when I deserved it)

To Mary Maier for the unique cover design

To my sister Bonnie and brother Gary who have helped
keep me as sane as possible for many years

The abbreviation HCP is sometimes used for High Card Points
"He" or "his" was used to make the book more readable.

"LHO" and "RHO" are abbreviations for Left Hand Opponent
and Right Hand Opponent.

Foreword

RANDY BARON and I go back quite a long way. We met more than 40 years ago. Randy had founded and was operating Baron Bridge Supply, which would grow to become the world's most successful retailer of bridge-related items. He lacked the time to play much — he was busy shipping bridge books, instructional software and teaching materials out the door — but he was a capable player and never lost his enthusiasm for the game and for enabling players to improve. Devyn Press, his publishing arm, issued dozens of books; in fact, Randy and I collaborated on a series of award-winning teaching manuals and student texts that are still used today.

Many years later, Randy sold his business, but his love affair with bridge remained. He combined his passion for travel — I don't think there is a part of the globe he has yet to visit — with a desire to help bridge players enjoy their favorite pastime: now Baron Bridge Travel coordinates trips tailored especially for them.

The book you are holding is unique. It is a distillation of Randy's vast experience as a player, as a frequent teacher and as someone whose knowledge of the literature of the game is unsurpassed. Randy has produced a treasury of tips — useful, practical advice, written with sincerity and with a deep respect and affection for the game and its beauties — that will benefit any player.

My friend Randy Baron's book is a worthy addition to the literature of bridge, and I feel honored that he asked me to write its Foreword.

—Frank Stewart

Introduction

"**B**RIDGE HAS BEEN very, very good to me," as Hall of Famer and humanitarian Roberto Clemente said about baseball. He is one of my true heroes, along with the Greatest-of-All-Time Muhammad Ali (proudly from my hometown of Louisville), Sister Helen Prejean (of "Dead Man Walking" fame), the Dalai Lama (a perfect role model and man of peace), Mr. Fred Rogers (Won't You Be My Neighbor?) and John Wooden (the incomparable UCLA coach). Since everyone has their problems and faults, it's difficult to rely on others as role models. However, I've been lucky that I was mentored by some of the best people and bridge personalities who have ever walked this earth: Easley Blackwood, Alfred Sheinwold, Edgar Kaplan, Bill Root, Dorothy and Alan Truscott and many others who helped me along the road of life. I could never overstate how important their assistance was to me. Besides being tremendous bridge players and writers, when I observed them, they always helped others. They were ethical and always tried to make the game better.

I've been playing bridge now for about 50 years and worn about every hat you can wear: expert (my partners might disagree), author, publisher, editor, columnist, teacher, politician, director, bridge club owner, and lately travel planner. In my 35 years as founder and president of Baron Barclay Bridge Supplies, the world's largest, I hope I've learned a few nuggets that will be useful to you. My intention is present to you a kind of Reader's Digest of essays and tips that can elevate your enjoyment and help you play with impeccable ethics.

There are many books and articles about how to improve your play, but there are few that focus on being a better partner, having fun and playing bridge the right way. In this book, there is plenty of technical advice. But more importantly, we'll examine the best ways to participate joyfully in the world's greatest game. In this time of various scandals at the highest levels of bridge, these topics need to be promoted more often. Besides, there are thousands of players around the world who have limited awareness that they are making unethical bids, plays or hesitations, or taking advantage of partner's actions.

Although you might have come across some of these tips in various books and magazine articles, I've tried to make this somewhat unique by focusing more on having a pleasant time playing and making your table a welcome and pleasant place to be. What's more important than being a positive role model for everyone around you and getting along with others and having a good time?

Most of the best players in the world are ladies and gentlemen at the table and have been from their earliest days in the game, but there have been too many high-level scandals. Luckily, Boye Brogeland of Norway and other notable experts have risked their reputations and spent countless hours trying to clean up the most prestigious events. It seems like we are headed in the right direction, so let's also make the experience more enjoyable for anyone who wants to play organized bridge. The ACBL has tried to foster such a setting with the Zero Tolerance

Policy, but most of the responsibility falls to the bridge club owners and directors. It's not easy...when I ran my bridge club after my college days, besides figuring out how to pay the bills, one of my most difficult decisions was how to handle the few players who caused problems at the table consistently.

You can choose which principles apply to you and your game. For example, I give advice to consider playing fewer complicated conventions to keep the game simpler. Later there are some recommended conventions I've played that you might want to consider, because they have been helpful to me. Much of what is appropriate for you to improve depends on your personality and how much work you want to put into being a better player, but as I have stressed throughout my book, you can always be a role model for those around you.

I hope that by reading my advice and sharing this with your partners and friends, we'll all be doing a little more to make the bridge world a friendlier and better environment. Thank you for the chance to share these tips with you.

IN LIFE AND BRIDGE, HAVE FUN! My favorite author, Joseph Campbell, expressed this best:

"Follow your bliss." and "Participate joyfully in the sorrows of the world."

Sincerely, Randy

Having Fun
and
Useful Habits

ONE

Be a Good Partner
BY MARTY BERGEN

"When One Great Scorer comes to write against your name, He marks, not that you won or lost, but how you played the game."

(One of my favorite quotes, expressed perfectly by Grantland Rice, a brilliant and renowned 20th Century sportswriter).

THE FOLLOWING 21 RULES from Marty Bergen (from his classic book "Points Schmoints" and reprinted in the *ACBL Bulletin*) give all players profound advice, simply and wisely. If these rules describe your regular partner or partners, please pat yourself and your partner on the back. If he has a few bad habits, maybe a copy of these rules will furnish a subtle hint to pay closer attention to them. If you cannot ever bring them to his attention or his behavior violates most of the rules, it's seriously time to wave good-bye, even if this is a difficult divorce.

21 Rules for being a good partner

Many years ago when doing the planning and research for what became my book "Points Schmoints," I compiled a list of rules for being a good partner. From what I have observed in the 20-plus years since then, there is no player in the world who would be hurt by reading and thinking about these guidelines.

I have also included several appropriate bridge quotes. The source for these was the excellent book "Classic Bridge Quotes" by Jared Johnson. Here is the most appropriate one:

"I have always believed that your attitude toward your partner is as important as your technical skill at the game."
—Rixi Markus, one of the all-time great players

I agree 100% with Ms. Markus on this topic: Half the battle in trying to win at bridge is being a good partner. Accordingly, I heartily recommend to all players to try very hard to always observe these rules:

1. Do not give lessons, unless you are being paid to do so. Even then, unless you are very sure that is the appropriate time and setting, think twice before sharing your "wisdom" with others.

    "According to an evening paper, there are only five real authorities on bridge in this country. Odd how often one gets one of them as a partner."
    — *Punch*, a British magazine.

2. Never say anything to your partner that you wouldn't want him to say to you. If you are even slightly unsure whether your partner would want you to say something, keep quiet.

3. Do not "result" — that is to say, do not criticize your partner for a normal action just because it didn't work this time.

4. Unless your intent is to clear up a misunderstanding, avoid discussing the hand just played. If you cannot resist, be discreet.

   In my partnership with Larry Cohen, we agreed to go even further. Since even an amicable discussion might distract one of us from concentrating 100% on the next boards, and the likelihood of the identical auction recurring during that session was small, we would refrain from clearing up the misunderstanding until after the session.

5. Remember that you and your partner are on the same team.

6. Don't forget that your partner wants to win as much as you do (even though sometimes his bid or play was so bizarre that it caused you to have serious doubts).

7. If you feel the urge to be nasty, sarcastic, critical or loud, excuse yourself and take a walk.

8. When there is time between hands, do not discuss bridge.

9. If you choose to ask another player about a disaster, ask about your hand, not your partner's.

10. Do not ever criticize or embarrass your partner in front of others.

11. Remember that bridge is only a game.

12. Have a good time, and make sure your partner does also. *"Bridge is for fun. You should play the game for no other reason. You should not play bridge to make money, to show how smart you are, or show how stupid your partner is... or to prove any of the several hundred other things bridge players are so often trying to prove."* —Bridge legend Charles Goren.

13. Trust your partner; do not assume he has made a mistake.

14. Although it may be unfashionable, it really is OK to be pleasant to a partner with whom you also happen to live.

15. Think before verbally analyzing a hand. Don't embarrass yourself with an inaccurate comment. *"The worst analysts and the biggest talkers are often one and the same."*— Columnist Frank Stewart.

16. When you voluntarily choose to play bridge with someone, it is not fair to get upset when partner does not play any better than usual.

17. Never side with an opponent against your partner. Either support your partner or say nothing.

18. If you think you are too good for a partner, and do not enjoy playing bridge with him, do everyone a favor and play with someone else. That is clearly much better than being a martyr. However, be careful before burning bridges — another player's grass may not be greener.

19. Learn your partner's style, regardless of how you feel about it. Do not expect your partner to bid exactly as

you would. When partner bids, consider what he will have, not what you would.

20. Picture problems from partner's point of view. Seek the bid or play that makes his life easiest.

21. Sympathize with partner if he makes a mistake. Let your partner know that you like him, and always root for him 100%.

MARTY BERGEN was voted one of the 25 most influential people in the history of bridge. He is a renowned teacher at all levels of the game and he has written over 60 popular books including "Points Schmoints," "Marty Sez" and "Better Bidding with Bergen," one of his earlier works which I enjoyed editing and publishing. Marty has had a regular column in the *ACBL Bulletin* for over 40 years, he's an ACBL Grand Life Master, and one of the leading theorists, developing many new conventions including Bergen Raises, DONT, and the Rule of 20.

The following is one of the best examples of how to be a good partner from the 1957 European Championships.

DEALER: North • VULNERABLE: North-South

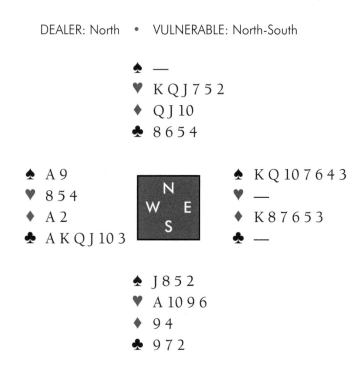

♠ —
♥ K Q J 7 5 2
♦ Q J 10
♣ 8 6 5 4

♠ A 9
♥ 8 5 4
♦ A 2
♣ A K Q J 10 3

♠ K Q 10 7 6 4 3
♥ —
♦ K 8 7 6 5 3
♣ —

♠ J 8 5 2
♥ A 10 9 6
♦ 9 4
♣ 9 7 2

NORTH	EAST	SOUTH	WEST
Jais	Forquet	Trezel	Siniscalco
(France)	(Italy)	(France)	(Italy)
1♥	4♠	Pass	4NT
Pass	6♦	Pass	6♠
Pass	7♠	Double	7NT
Double	All pass		

Trezel's double of 7♠ betrayed the trump position, giving Forquet a chance to make his contract. Forquet's partner,

Siniscalco ran to 7NT and he lost the first six heart tricks. Italy recovered and won the match, due largely to Forquet's ability to deal with the disaster. He didn't say a word and simply went on to the next hand. His behavior enabled his partner to recover his composure and play well for the rest of the match.

Out of all the experts in the 1950s and 1960s, one of the most popular was Howard Schenken. He was always a gentleman and virtually everyone wanted to play with him. They explained that they had a big edge because they were Howard's favorite partner. Each of his "favorite partners" played well when they sat across from him.

Here are two more quotes, one on how to think at the table and one on a habit to avoid:

> "Never reproach your partner if there is the slightest thing for which you can reproach yourself. "
> —Ely Culbertson

> "It's always partner's fault."
> —The First Rule of Bridge

I'll close this principle with an old joke for two reasons. It's a funny story and it also has an important message about being a good partner and having fun at the table...

Sheryl accompanied Wayne, her bridge partner, to the doctor's office. After his checkup, the doctor called Sheryl into his office alone. "Wayne is suffering from a severe stress disorder. If you don't follow my instructions carefully, he will surely die. Never point out any mistake he makes. Be pleasant at all times. Don't burden him with conventions and bidding systems. Always give him a hug when he feels down. And never discuss the hands. If you can do this for the next few months, I think Wayne will regain his health completely."

On the way home, Wayne asked Sheryl, "What did the doctor say?"

With a wink and a smile, Sheryl replied, "He said you are going to die." (Courtesy of Brent Manley and the *ACBL Bulletin*)

♠ ♡ ◇ ♣

TWO

Choose Your Partners Wisely

"Avoid the company of deluded people when you can. When you cannot, keep your own counsel."

–Jack Kornfield

MY ADVICE TO YOU is simple. Play only with partners you like, enjoy and respect. Your partner should be someone you enjoy sitting across the table from. There are many good reasons to spend a session with someone: their personality, a cooperative and winning partnership, and a chance to learn or to share your wisdom. Perhaps your partner is pretty or handsome (a boost for your ego), or a long list of reasons not mentioned here.

Life is too short (at the bridge table or anywhere else) to have to tolerate a mean, unfriendly, unethical, ill-tempered, pompous person for three or four hours for a session of bridge. If you are playing all day together at a tournament or for several days, why would you ever subject yourself to such a partner? For a team game when you have three teammates, it's even more insane unless you are a masochist.

In my early days of bridge, my ego sometimes demanded that I play with various partners and on teams when I never felt comfortable. Winning or at least having the best team possible was my goal. Although I achieved success frequently, I realized that I wasn't having fun a majority of the time. When you are playing with a person or persons you don't like or respect as a fellow human being, it takes away from this beautiful game of bridge. You usually don't play your best and the level of stress is higher when you don't have a reasonable relationship with your partner.

One of the intangibles that makes bridge unique is the importance of good chemistry between partners. Everything that happens within your partnership can affect how well you do. It's more than your individual technical skills and depth of partnership understanding. It's also your will to win, your mental stamina and your morale. So what can be more important than having someone who appreciates and understands you sitting across from you at the table?

This principle, as well as being a good partner, is the most important in this book. Please take this to heart, so you will do your small part in making the bridge club or tournament, and the world a better place for everyone.

I'll close with another one of my favorite quotes:

"The purpose of life is joy."
—Gill Edwards

♠ ♡ ◇ ♣

THREE

Always Follow The Golden Rule: Treat Your Partner, Opponents, Directors and Everyone You Come in Contact with as You Wish to Be Treated

"No act of kindness, no matter how small, is ever wasted."

–Aesop

HOPEFULLY you have already taken this to heart early in your bridge career. However, like all invaluable wisdom in life, you cannot hear this too often.

I have already shared Marty Bergen's "21 Rules of Being a Good Partner." You should realize (if you haven't thought about it before) that you come in contact with many others at the bridge club or tournament. If you play 26 boards (an average number for most events), you will play against 26 opponents (13 rounds with two new opponents per round).

13

Besides treating everyone at the table with respect, why not go even further? Greet each person with a sincere hello and introduce yourselves if you haven't met the opponents. Many of the successful bridge clubs now have name badges available to make it easier to acknowledge who you are playing against; these badges are also helpful if you have seen your opponents previously, but can't remember their names. That's a welcome benefit as we age and our memories aren't perfect.

There are additional small gestures you can make, so that everyone feels welcome. Several regulars at my home club in Louisville bring candy and offer it to everyone who arrives at their table or when they come to a table as east-west.

If there's time at the end of the round, it's fun to share stories or current events (remember the old brilliant advice: stay away from politics and religion unless you know someone well...here in Kentucky or in North Carolina your basketball team can be even more polarizing than other subjects, so choose your comments wisely).

♠ ♡ ◇ ♣

FOUR

Always Be an Ethical Player. It's Much More Important than Winning

BY DENNY & JERRY CLERKIN

"How we respond to a game tells more about us than real life."

–Captain Jean-Luc Picard,
"Star Trek, the Next Generation"

ETHICAL CONDUCT is defined as conforming to accepted virtuous, moral standards of conduct and, of course, everyone should strive their best to always follow the rules of bridge. The good news is that a vast majority of players want to enjoy a fun, fair game and being ethical is the way they behave. The bad news is that some players, because of lack of education, violate rules and don't ever realize they are doing it. We'll try to explain some of the most frequent violations of these principles, so you will know when you are being as ethical as possible.

Unfortunately, at the highest levels of bridge there have been a number of high-profile scandals. As in professional sports and the Olympics, there is much glory and money at stake. A few bad apples always try to win through cheating and unethical conduct. Through intense efforts by some of the best players in the world and modern technology (video recording), the tournament world has made remarkable strides in recent years.

You should understand that in some card games like poker, all sorts of gamesmanship are tolerated or even welcomed. In bridge, a strict code of ethics and courtesy is part of the game. The higher the standard of play, the higher the standard of ethics is demanded. If you are playing in a social game at home, you can certainly have a more informal atmosphere, but it's still helpful for everyone to understand the proper way to play.

We're much more concerned about making sure that games at the clubs are as fair as possible. Here's what you should know to help you follow the laws in the proper way: not only ethics, but also proper conduct and etiquette.

There are various kinds of behavior that are obviously inappropriate:

- Upsetting the opponents in any way to make them play badly.
- Looking into an opponent's hand to see one or more cards (even if they don't hold their cards back).
- Varying the normal tempo of bidding or play for the purpose of disconcerting the other players.

- Using different designations for the same call such as "A club" or "I'll bid one club," instead of the correct "One club." (Most clubs and tournaments use bidding boxes now, so this is much less of a problem than it used to be. If you play at home or in an informal group, it's a good idea to explain this to your guests).
- Indicating any approval or disapproval of a call or play. (We are constantly surprised by this violation by players with thousands of masterpoints. They will frown or glare when they are displeased by a play, while looking happy if they are satisfied with the way the play is going, especially on defense).
- Indicating the expectation or intention of winning or losing a trick before play to that trick has been completed.
- Commenting or acting during the auction or play to call attention to the number of tricks that will be required for success.
- Looking intently at any other player during the auction or play.
- Observing the place from which a player draws a card.
- Making any special emphasis, gesture or mannerism.
- It is improper for communication between partners to be affected by the questions asked of the opponents or explanations given to them.
- It is improper to have any special understandings regarding your bids and plays of which the opponents aren't aware.

I hope you and your friends have fun by always:

- Playing only with people you like
- Being good partners
- Being ethical and behaving properly

(The appendix includes an essay by Robb Gordon, *ACBL National Recorder*, about the concept of "Active Ethics.")

DENNY and **JERRY CLERKIN** were born in the small Indiana town of North Vernon. They have won 18 National Championships, hundreds of Regionals, and have represented the USA in the World Championships numerous times. The Clerkins still compete full-time as professionals and teach in Indianapolis and South Florida. Even though bridge is a serious game, they have a perfect attitude at the table, trying their hardest to win, but also having fun and sharing laughs.

RANDY: Their most important contribution (besides this principle) is their insight at our monthly book club for over 20 years.

♠ ♡ ◇ ♣

FIVE

Make Sure You Pause After a Skip Bid by the Opponents

"Madam, that second hesitation was certainly an overbid."

–Charles Goren

A S I HAVE EXPRESSED throughout this book, besides being a good partner, opponent and human being, the next most important trait to have in life and at the bridge table is to be ethical at all times.

Even though the Stop card was eliminated from bidding boxes at the start of 2018, you are still obligated to pause whenever the opponent who bids just before your turn makes a skip bid (for example, opening 3♣). This will avoid giving unauthorized information to your partner. You should also try to maintain an even tempo during the auction.

The appropriate action is to wait about ten seconds before making any call, whether it's a pass, double or bid. It's also crucial that you wait the same ten seconds (and you can take longer if you have a problem) whether you have zero points or a monster hand. It's not OK to pass quickly (as many players do) when you aren't planning to bid. And you should look at your hand the same way whether you will pass or bid; the opponents and your partner should not be able to obtain information from your manner as you wait the ten seconds.

Obviously, you shouldn't close your eyes and count without looking at your cards or use any other method to show that you have no intention of doing anything except passing.

If the opponents receive information from you, they are entitled to it and can use your mannerisms to their advantage during the deal. However, your partner is absolutely not entitled to this information and that is why you should be careful to be consistent in this situation. Make sure you remember this every time there is a skip bid and you'll be playing the game the correct way.

♠ ♡ ◇ ♣

SIX

Familiarize Yourself with the Laws of Bridge

BY ROBB GORDON

"Ignorance of the law excuses no man."

–John Selden

I T'S SURPRISING how many players know so little about the laws, their ignorance evident when the director is called to the table. There are numerous times when a reasonable knowledge of the laws can really help you. Knowing your rights and making the best choice when you have options are crucial parts of being a winning player and partnership.

I have listed some of the most significant and frequent topics that are important for you to understand (I won't discuss every detail, but I will give you a brief idea of laws and issues that appear often...there are various books written about the laws and behavioral problems, and there is a wealth of information on the ACBL website where you can search for "Laws").

1. Whenever there is an irregularity at the table or you think there could be a problem, always call the director to your table by the words, "Director, please." This is the proper way to ask; it never hurts to be a lady or a gentleman, especially when you are playing bridge. Many inexperienced players are petrified when the director is called, but it's simply part of the game. No matter your level of expertise and what has happened, be pleasant and allow the director to ask the proper questions. For example, one of the irregularities that occurs often is an opening lead out of turn. Declarer has five choices available to him. There is nothing to be worried or ashamed about, because it can happen to anyone. When your partnership makes a lead out of turn, simply vow to concentrate more and avoid this in the future.

2. The ACBL's Zero Tolerance policy: The league is attempting to eliminate unacceptable behavior and to make clubs and tournaments friendly without rude, disruptive behavior (There is an essay about Zero Tolerance in the appendix).

3. The procedure following a ruling and your right to appeal.

4. Your options when there is a lead out of turn.

5. What happens when there is a revoke.

6. What you should do when your opponents bid out of tempo (fast or slow) or transmit other unintentional unauthorized information.

7. Laws concerning penalty cards (declarer cannot have a penalty card).

8. Laws concerning insufficient bids.
9. Laws when there is a pass or bid out of turn.
10. Dummy's rights
11. Adjusted scores
12. Slow play
13. Claims

ROBB GORDON grew up in Livonia, Michigan and now lives in Prescott, Arizona. He may be the only living person who played with Charles Goren and John Gerber. His parents were active in bridge, so when he was eight, Robb was at a Regional. He took his cars and trucks to the lobby of the hotel, where he recruited Goren and Gerber to play with his toys! Robb became a Life Master at 20 and has won over 100 Regionals, as well as a National Championship. He serves on the Laws Commission and is currently the National Recorder for the ACBL.

SEVEN

When You Are Dummy, Be the Best Dummy You Can Be

"You shouldn't be proud of doing the right thing. You should just do it."

—Dean Smith, legendary North Carolina Tar Heel coach (if you enjoy entertaining sports books, obtain a copy of "The Legends Club" by John Feinstein, at the top of the list of sports writers. Even if you aren't a fan of Duke, NC or NC State, it's a very human story, worth your time. I promise).

WHEN YOU ARE DUMMY, it's a good time to relax and take advantage of the fact that you don't have to play a contract or defend. However, to be a good dummy there are various duties you can perform to help your partner:

- When you spread the dummy, put down the suit that was led by the opponents last. This is a subtle way to ensure that declarer doesn't play from dummy until he studies the hand (see my Principle #13 in Volume 2 about thinking before you play to trick one as declarer).

- Space the cards neatly, so the other three players can see all 13 cards in the dummy clearly with the suits alternated by colors.
- Make sure you are aware which hand declarer should be leading from and alert him if you think he is about to try to lead from the wrong hand.
- Make sure your partner follows suit. Ask, "No spades, partner?" to ensure he is void in a suit when he ruffs in his hand. This avoids a revoke.
- Dummy should keep track of each trick accurately, so when the play is over, he knows the exact result of the hand.
- At the end of the hand but not before, dummy may draw attention to any errors in play (such as a revoke) or if someone has violated a law during the play.
- Dummy may give information in the director's presence, as to facts of what occurred at the table.

There are limitations to what dummy is allowed to do:

- Dummy may not initiate a call for the director during play unless another player has drawn attention to an irregularity.
- Dummy may not call attention to an irregularity during play.
- Dummy must not participate in the play or communicate about the play to declarer.
- Dummy may not exchange hands with declarer or leave his seat to watch declarer's play of the hand.

- Dummy may not look at the face of a card in either defender's hand and a defender is not allowed to show dummy his hand.

There are penalties for any violation of these laws.

♠ ♡ ◇ ♣

EIGHT

Ask Questions at the Proper Time

"To everything there is a season, and a time to every purpose under heaven."

–Ecclesiastes 3:1

INEXPERIENCED PLAYERS are sometimes overwhelmed by the seemingly countless issues they have to deal with at the table. They are trying to understand the bidding, play, defense, etiquette, laws and so much more. Although there is a learning curve for our game, here is simple advice that is easy to follow:

When the opponents are involved in an uncontested auction, don't ask questions until the auction is over. This is a bad move that happens frequently and it's unnecessary. Not only does it assist the opponents when they aren't sure about their bids, but it can also complicate the auction by giving partner unauthorized information. When you have no intention of making a call during the auction, it is always best to stay silent instead of asking questions. Asking before the auction is over interferes with the opponents' tempo, as well as their concentration during the bidding. It can create problems and tension, as well as slowing down the game for no reason.

A much better method of finding out what the opponents' bids mean is to wait until the auction ends or you can look at their convention card. Before making the opening lead, you can ask about their entire auction or the meaning of a specific bid (although it's better to request a review of everything, so you don't draw attention to a particular call that gives unauthorized information to your partner). Your partner also has that right, so make your lead face down to allow him a chance to ask about the auction.

Here's more helpful advice about players' rights:

- During the play, either defender may request an explanation of a bid, so it's not only limited to the period before the opening lead (however, players are entitled to a full review of the auction only before they play to trick one).
- Whenever it's declarer's turn to play from either hand, he may ask about a defender's bid or carding agreements.
- Before the opening lead, it's a good idea for the declarer's side to voluntarily explain a complicated auction without being asked by the defenders.
- Even though it's not required, when opponents arrive at the table, it's suggested that each pair disclose if they are playing an unusual bidding system or using non-standard discarding.

♠ ♡ ◇ ♣

NINE

Decide Why You Choose to Play the Game

"Figuring out what you truly want in life is difficult. Achieving it, by comparison, is easy."

—Unknown author

HERE ARE SOME common reasons why people play bridge. Take a few minutes to consider why you play. Understanding this motivation will help you learn a little more about yourself.

- Ego gratification
- Competition
- Winning
- Having fun
- Learning a new skill
- Solving problems
- Interacting with people
- Helping our memory as we age
- Finding someone to have a relationship with or to date
- Making contacts for your business
- Because your spouse/significant other wants to play

- Because your spouse/significant other doesn't want to play (so it's a good excuse to have a little time away from each other)
- To earn money as a director, author, bridge club owner, professional, selling bridge items, or teacher
- It's inexpensive entertainment.
- It's become a habit.

♠ ♡ ◇ ♣

TEN

Learn The Game; Don't Worry About Winning or How Many Masterpoints You Have Accumulated

"Success is a journey, not a destination. The doing is often more important than the outcome."

—Arthur Ashe, one of the best role models
of the 20th Century

I HAVE MET MANY PLAYERS over the years who are obsessed with winning events and tallying as many masterpoints as possible. Let me give you a little advice: Although everyone likes to emerge victorious when competing at bridge or other games, don't make this your main goal.

If you work at becoming a better player, the championships and masterpoints will take care of themselves. If you play long enough, you'll earn plenty of points and, unlike chess, once you have your points, they are yours forever.

It might help to point out a few facts that should be obvious.

1. You cannot sell your points...as my grandfather used to say, that and a nickel will buy you a cup of coffee (now it's more like $5 than a nickel).
2. Like your bank account, you can't take the points with you when you go to the ultimate bridge game in heaven (if you have followed my principles about proper behavior, you should at least have a decent chance).

So relax, enjoy the game and the friends you have made. If you are never a world or national champion, your dog, cat, pot-bellied pig and your family will still love you when you return home.

A final thought on this subject: The less you assume you know, the more you can learn.

♠ ♡ ◇ ♣

ELEVEN

Hold Your Cards So the Opponents Can't See Them

"The unfortunate thing about this world is that good habits are much easier to give up than bad ones."

—Somerset Maugham

AT CLUBS AND TOURNAMENTS, I'm often amazed at how many seemingly intelligent players allow their opponents to see all or part of their hands. I'm not exaggerating when I tell you that in 13 rounds of bridge (if we are playing two boards against each opponent) there will be an average of three or four players who commit this error. Shockingly, many of these opponents have been playing for years; these are open games, not novice competitions. It's certainly a much more serious problem than most people and directors realize, especially with older players who tend to let their guard down (they are simply concerned with counting their points and sorting the suits correctly).

So I make the proper comment in a friendly way, "Please hold your cards back." However, most of the time they will continue to show their cards. Not only does it hurt their score; it allows the pairs sitting your way to take advantage (not everyone does, but it happens) and it affects your matchpoints.

- If you partner tends to show his cards, make sure that you point this out to him.
- If an opponent does this, tell him or her in a kind way to pay attention and hold back the cards.
- If you are a director, you can talk in private to the players who show their cards and possibly make an announcement occasionally to alert everyone to try to eliminate this mistake.

Let's all do our part to make bridge a fairer and more ethical game.

♠ ♡ ◇ ♣

TWELVE

During the Play, Make Sure the Opponents Can't Tell Your Distribution

"The first step toward winning at bridge is to become not only suspicious and watchful of others, but also to realize that for the most part, you are playing with a group of people who have the instinct of ax murderers."

–Jerry Sohl (my all-time favorite bridge quote)

WE ALL HAVE HABITS we develop over the years, away from the bridge table and while we're playing. Most are harmless or, at the worst, annoying. However, have you ever given much thought to how you sort your cards or where you take the cards from during the play of the hand?

Almost all of us sort the cards into four suits after we remove the hand from the duplicate board. That's perfectly fine, because this makes counting your points and learning your distribution easier. There is no reason to change this habit while you are bidding the hand.

It's an entirely different story once the bidding is over. Whether you are declarer or defender, it's important to keep your distribution a secret as much as possible.

Many of the top players don't keep their cards sorted into suits during the play of the hand for this reason. It's a great idea to keep your cards in some random order, because if you don't, opponents can see where you pull a card from and take advantage of you.

Which player has a queen or which way to take a finesse is often the difference between a top or bottom, or winning a match in a team game.

So be aware of this. It's a topic that most people don't consider and it can make you a winner or an also-ran.

♠ ♡ ◇ ♣

THIRTEEN

Table Talk and Tells: Your Opponents Are Talking, You Are Listening

BY MIKE WOLF

"A wise old owl lived in an oak,
The more he saw the less he spoke.
The less he spoke the more he heard;
Why can't we all be like this wise old bird?"

"Loose lips sink ships" (or "beware unguarded talk")
was part of a general campaign during World War
II to advise servicemen and other citizens to avoid
careless talk concerning secure information that
might be of use to the enemy. Bridge players would
be well advised to heed this advice.

MORE PREVALENT in social games and club duplicate games than at serious tournaments (but still very common in that venue as well), is the propensity of players to make faces, gripe, complain, or admonish partner during the bidding or on defense, and when putting down the dummy. Much can be learned by just looking and listening.

Good defenders can be double dummy given extraneous information. For example, you hold as East, playing matchpoints:

♠ Q 9 x x
♥ J x x x
♦ x x
♣ A x x

The auction by the opponents has proceeded:

NORTH	SOUTH
1♥	1NT
3NT	

Partner leads the 10 of clubs, and as North puts down the dummy, South who is in the habit of doing this, comments about each suit as follows:

Spades "not so good"
Hearts "good"
Diamonds "nice"
Clubs "okay"

The dummy is:

♠ J x x
♥ A K 9 8 7
♦ A x
♣ K Q J

When you win the A of clubs at trick one, what do you play? Spades looks like it could be a frozen suit (This is when none of the players can attack the suit for their benefit; there is a very helpful article in the July, 2013 *ACBL Bulletin* on this subject by Eddie Kantar), hearts are out of the question, diamonds could be right, clubs look safe. Well, the declarer told you what to play, didn't he?

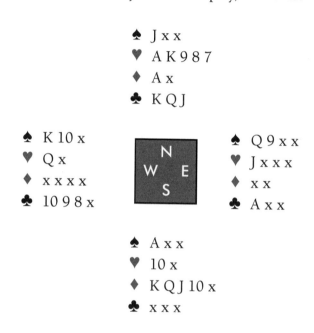

```
                    ♠ J x x
                    ♥ A K 9 8 7
                    ♦ A x
                    ♣ K Q J

♠ K 10 x                           ♠ Q 9 x x
♥ Q x              N                ♥ J x x x
♦ x x x x      W       E            ♦ x x
♣ 10 9 8 x         S                ♣ A x x

                    ♠ A x x
                    ♥ 10 x
                    ♦ K Q J 10 x
                    ♣ x x x
```

Without a spade return, declarer has 11 tricks, as he has time to set up hearts and loses only a club and heart. With the spade return, declarer is held to 10 tricks if he cashes out. (Otherwise, he'll make less).

You'll be amazed at how many extra tricks you will garner simply by paying attention to opponents' mannerisms, comments and expressions.

MIKE WOLF learned bridge in 1970 at the University of Arizona. He then concentrated on his family and law practice, before making the game a priority in recent years. Mike teaches weekly classes at the Ft. Lauderdale Bridge Club and plays professionally in South Florida. He has dozens of regional titles to his credit and finished 2nd in two national events in 2017.

RANDY: Although comments such as those illustrated in the above example are frowned upon and should be avoided, they do occur occasionally (especially when the players know each other well at the club and the atmosphere is very informal). This principle is included so you will realize how important it is to behave properly at the table. Follow all guidelines for etiquette and ethics; also, you can improve your scores by not giving away information to the opponents.

♤ ♡ ◇ ♧

FOURTEEN

Relax and Keep Your Wits When Things Aren't Going Well

"Don't give up ... don't ever give up."

—Jim Valvano, N.C. State basketball coach

THIS IS AN EXTENSION of the principle of both partners always being supportive of each other, no matter what has happened during the current session. If you keep a positive attitude and don't criticize each other, it's much easier to treat each hand as a separate competition without dwelling on something negative.

You also don't know what is happening at other tables (or at the other table if you are playing in a team game). We've all had days when we were surprised or shocked at our results; so if you just keep plugging away, doing the best you can on every board, you might be rewarded handsomely for your efforts. And no one likes to play with a partner with a bad attitude.

The bottom line: there is no good reason to act like a spoiled brat or a down-in-the-dumps partner. Stay positive and keep trying your best.

FIFTEEN

Take a Deep Breath

"Guts is grace under pressure."

–Ernest Hemingway

WHEN YOU ARE in a stressful, pressure situation at the bridge table, take a deep breath or two. Try to give yourself a few extra moments to calm down. You have probably seen athletes in every major sport follow this valuable advice. On a good day, you might find yourself with a chance to win an event or a match. This can be a very intimidating time, especially if you've seldom been there before. Concentrate to the best of your ability and remember that it's only a game. No matter what happens, your family still loves you (I hope), you still have your health, and the sun will shine again tomorrow (assuming it's not winter and you don't live in the frozen tundra in the north).

This excellent advice comes from one of America's top experts, Steve Weinstein, who suggests this strategy on his video on the Bridge Winners website. When we are nervous, we tend to bid or play quickly, when the opposite is probably better.

From the Rudyard Kipling poem "If":

If you can keep your head when all about you
    Are losing theirs and blaming it on you;
If you can trust yourself when all men doubt you,
    But make allowance for their doubting too.
If you can wait and not be tired by waiting,
    Or being lied about, don't deal in lies,
Or being hated, don't give way to hating,
    And yet don't look too good, nor talk too wise.

If you can talk with crowds and keep your virtue,
    Or walk with Kings—nor lose the common touch,
If neither foes nor loving friends can hurt you,
    If all men count with you, but none too much;
If you can fill the unforgiving minute
    With sixty seconds' worth of distance run,
Yours is the Earth and everything that's in it,
    And—which is more—you'll be a Man, my son!

♠ ♡ ◇ ♣

SIXTEEN

Ecstasy

BY MIKE LAWRENCE

"I've got a beautiful feelin'. Everything's going my way."

—Oscar Hammerstein

ALMOST EVERYONE I KNOW will admit to the following mishap. You are declaring, say, 3NT and due to unfortunate circumstances, the defenders are running their five-card suit so you are going down at least one. Being depressed about bidding, you discard poorly thus messing up your entries. Suddenly, your eight remaining tricks become only six when the opponents take advantage of your sloppy carding. Three down. It's bad enough you're getting a zero, but even with your head hung half-way to the floor, you catch a glimpse of partner whispering to his kibitzer.

Sound familiar?

Bad news is infectious. It brings with it emotions ranging from disappointment to sadness to depression, any one of which can distract and cause muddled thinking.

Most players know that it is important to keep your wits when things go sour. The trick is to recognize when your concentration is failing and to get your thoughts back together.

The tough player does this automatically. The good player struggles, but usually succeeds and the rest of the world does it occasionally, but not routinely. You say "I KNOW THAT." I agree that you probably do know that, but do you really know it on a usable conscious level?

Strong negative emotions obstruct our thoughts.

Is there anything worse for our emotions than bad news? Try this.

The bidding goes 1NT, pass, 3NT. You lead fourth best from K-J-8-6-4-2. Dummy has two small spades and twelve high-card points.

Have you led into the A-Q? No. Partner plays the ace and starts to think. Does he have another spade? Is he thinking of switching? Partner, lead a spade! Please! Partner leads — the 10. You are now in charge with six running spades which you proceed to take. Each one a little firmer than the one before, you pound out your remaining spades, the last one being especially satisfying because it is getting you plus two hundred.

You're feeling a little ecstasy mixed with a little power as you turn the final spade. Feels good doesn't it?

Now what? Cutting through a euphoric glow, you reconstruct the last four tricks. Let's see now. Partner discarded the — what did he discard? I know his last card was the 7. But the one before that, and the one before that... Come to think of it, what did dummy discard, or for that matter declarer?

Do you think you're going to get it right? What if part-ner has another ace and you don't get it? Can you stand to see partner talking to that kibitzer again?

Ecstasy plays no favorites. It muddles your bidding judgment, your declarer play and your defensive aware-ness with equal facility.

DEALER: East • VULNERABLE: Both sides

♠ 9 5
♥ K Q 6 2
♦ A 10
♣ A J 9 6 3

♠ Q J 8
♥ J 9 5
♦ K Q 7 3
♣ K Q 4

WEST	NORTH	EAST	SOUTH
–	–	Pass	1♦
Pass	2♣	Pass	2NT
Pass	3♥	Pass	3NT
All pass			

West leads the ♠6 to East's ace. This is your basic dull contract which looks like a routine nine tricks. Perhaps you have been unlucky to get a spade lead. For instance, if North hadn't bid 3♥, you might have gotten a heart lead allowing you ten tricks. Therefore, when East returns a spade ducked by West, you have to consider whether to finesse the ♦10 in order to try for ten tricks.

First, just to put your mind at ease, you cash the ♣K. West pitches the ♥3.

Eight fast tricks. Not nine. So where is the ninth coming from? You have two possible plays.

1. Play on Hearts and hope Spades are 4-4.
2. Finesse the 10 of diamonds.

Which play is right?

The answer depends on your opinion of the spades. If East returned the two, the suit rates to be 4-4 in which case, you should play on hearts. If East returned a higher spade, then spades are likely to be 5-3 in which case you have to hope for the diamond finesse.

The issue here is very simple. Either you paid attention to the spade spots and made an educated decision or you didn't pay attention to the spade spots and therefore had to make an uneducated guess. If you allowed the comfort of nine apparent tricks to cloud your vision, you're in trouble. Conversely, if you ignored emotional intrusions and paid attention to the cards, then you were able to determine rather than to guess the correct play.

My **BOLS TIP** is: Anytime you feel yourself succumbing to an emotion, whether sadness, depression, irritation, COMFORT, ELATION or ECSTASY, you should fight it off. STOP AND PAY ATTENTION!

MIKE LAWRENCE is one of the world's great players who lives in Tennessee with his wife, Karen. He was an original member of the famed Dallas Aces and won two Bermuda Bowls with them. Mike has since then won another World Championship and holds 16 National titles. He is an acclaimed author with more than 25 books to his credit.

RANDY: I had the good fortune to edit and publish twelve of Mike's classic books including "How to Read the Opponents' Cards," "Judgment at Bridge," "Overcalls" and "Dynamic Defense." Working with Mike was always a joy and I appreciate all of his hard work that helped put my children through college.

♠ ♡ ◇ ♣

SEVENTEEN

The Harder You Practice, the Luckier You Get

"Luck is where preparation meets opportunity."

–Anonymous

THE TITLE OF THIS PRINCIPLE has been uttered by countless top athletes, including Michael Jordan and Gary Player. It's true about bridge, like any activity you enjoy. I'm sure you have seen many players who come to your club or to a tournament week after week without attempting to learn anything new. Although there is certainly nothing wrong with embracing the social aspect of our game, they simply do the best they can and are usually satisfied with the results. Whatever you devote your time to, why not strive to be the best you can be? It doesn't matter whether it's your family, occupation or playing a sport or game. Try to balance your bridge hours between playing, reading books and articles, improving your partnership(s), and evaluating your past results.

Because of the miracles of modern technology, you can play bridge 24 hours a day if you don't need to eat, sleep, take care of family obligations, or bring home a paycheck. Partners are available anytime you are in the mood to compete online. At 3 A.M. your time, you can join a table comprised of players from New Zealand, Pakistan and Mongolia, or anywhere else where they have a computer and access to Bridge Base Online.

There are countless hands to bid with your regular partner in magazines and on your computer, as well as hundreds of books with bidding, play and defensive problems. Take a close look at where you could use improvement and vow to learn as much as possible.

I'll close with a profound thesis that Malcolm Gladwell proposes in his #1 bestseller "Outliers." He claims that the key to achieving world-class expertise in any skill is practicing for about 10,000 hours. If Bill Gates and the Beatles could become so proficient in business and music, maybe you have enough time to practice bridge for that long and become a world-class expert.

EIGHTEEN

Respect Everyone, Fear No One
BY DR. LEE BUKSTEL

"Figuring the players is as important as figuring the cards."

—Easley Blackwood, inventor of the world's most popular and most abused convention

WHETHER YOU ARE PLAYING against world champions or beginners at your club who just finished their first set of lessons, try to remain relaxed but competitive. Try not to be intimidated by players who you know are better than you are; do not become cocky and overly confident against players who are not as skilled as you are. At whatever level you play, "Respect everyone, fear no one" can be your private bridge mantra to keep you focused. It can alleviate any unwanted tension, timidity or an arrogant attitude.

Against top experts or the best players at your club, you can expect to suffer some poor results. They not only keep their mistakes to a minimum, but they also find creative ways in the bidding and play to make your life difficult. It's a tough combination: great technique, total concentration and aggressive bidding. Even though the odds are stacked against you, try your best, concentrate and focus to the best of your ability. Don't be afraid to make a great bid or play.

It's easy to be intimidated, even if you are an experienced player. I was playing in a Florida Regional in the top flight where every team except ours had multiple world and national champions. Twice during the event, a well-known player bid game in a competitive auction. Both times my partner would have automatically doubled against any pair below the world class level. Against these top players, he passed meekly both times. One of these errors kept us from winning the match. Since then, he has vowed not to allow that to happen again.

At the other end of the spectrum, it can be an opportunity for easy success when an inexperienced pair is your opponent. Sure, you can be more aggressive than usual in competitive auctions; they probably won't double you and sometimes you can steal a good result. You can also frequently find a way to win an extra trick or they will go down in a cold contract. But be careful not to be too smug or too confident and act like your opponent is always there for the taking. The card gods don't appreciate that and karma can sometimes rear its head in the swish of a horse's tail.

In summary, maintain an even keel. Most champion athletes never get too high or too low, no matter what has happened. They keep playing their game, whether it's against a worthy opponent or someone they expect to defeat.

DR. LEE BUKSTEL of Boca Raton, Florida started playing bridge at the University of Florida in 1969 with a group of friends in his fraternity. He took a 20-year break to concentrate on his psychology practice and to become an avid SCUBA diver. Lee has appeared on the Barry Crane 500 list twice and has placed 2nd in two 0-10,000 national events. Besides representing Florida multiple times in the Grand National Teams, he has captured many regional and sectional titles.

RANDY: Even though Lee takes the game seriously, he is a perfect example of how to act at the table. Because we have fun, I consider him one of the best partners in the country. We greet our opponents with a smile and a warm welcome; then we seek to win as much as anyone. I was one of the players in his fraternity house. Lee and another of our brothers there have been my best friends in the world for over 50 years. Our motto, "Not four years, but a lifetime" was completely appropriate for us. By the way, I was that partner who "forgot" to double in Florida on those hands. Despite those results and numerous vulnerable light overcalls that I have made, Lee still plays with me as much as possible.

NINETEEN

Include at Least Several Declarer Play Books in Your Personal Library and Take Time to Learn from the Example Hands

"I'm quite illiterate, but I read a lot."

–J.D. Salinger

BIDDING AND DEFENSE are essential to becoming a better player, but they require partnership discussion and cooperation. However, your declarer play can be improved by simply studying hands from the best books on the subject. There are many that are helpful and I will recommend four of my favorites: Bill Root's "How to Play a Bridge Hand," Mollo & Gardener's "Card Play Technique," Barbara Seagram and David Bird's "25 Ways to Take More Tricks as Declarer," and Larry Cohen's "Larry Teaches Declarer Play." You can set up the hands at home by taking a deck of cards, dealing them out and going through the play trick by trick. Then you'll recognize these situations when they occur at the table.

Along with the books already mentioned, I have included a list of some of my favorite books that I have appreciated and read over the years. There are many others that will help you improve and I apologize in advance if your favorites are not on my list. Also note that some of these titles are currently out of print, so obtaining a copy might not be easy.

A FEW OF MY FAVORITE BRIDGE BOOKS

1 = Advanced Beginners
2 = Intermediate
3 = Advanced
4 = All players

1, 2	Bergen: *Points Schmoints*
1	Blackwood & Hanson: *Card Play Fundamentals*
4	Cohen: *Larry Teaches Declarer Play*
4	Cohen: *Larry Teaches 2 over 1 Game Forcing*
2, 3	Cohen: *To Bid or Not To Bid (The Law of Total Tricks)*
4	Darvas & de V. Hart: *Right Through the Pack*
4	Ewen: *Opening Leads*
1, 2	Grant: *Popular Conventions*
2, 3	Grant & Rodwell: *2 over 1 Game Force*
1, 2	Hardy & Bruno: *2 over 1, An Introduction*
2, 3	Kantar: *Advanced Bridge Defense*
1, 2	Kantar: *Modern Bridge Defense*
3	Kelsey: *Killing Defense*
2, 3	Klinger: *100 Winning Duplicate Tips*
1, 2	Lampert: *The Fun Way to Advanced Bridge*

4	Lawrence: *Dynamic Defense*
4	Lawrence: *How to Read Your Opponents' Cards*
4	Lawrence: *Judgment at Bridge*
3	Love: *Bridge Squeezes Complete*
3	Mollo: *Bridge in the Menagerie*
2, 3	Mollo & Gardener: *Card Play Technique*
3	Reese: *Master Play*
1, 2	Root: *Commonsense Bidding*
1, 2	Root: *How to Play a Bridge Hand*
4	Root & Pavlicek: *Modern Bridge Conventions*
3	Rubens: *Secrets of Winning Bridge*
4	Seagram & Smith: *25 Conventions You Should Know*
4	Seagram & Smith: *25 Ways to Compete in the Bidding*
4	Seagram & Smith: *25 Ways to Take More Tricks as Declarer*
4	Simon: *Why You Lose at Bridge*
1, 2	Stewart: *Comprehensive Guide to Defense*
4	Stewart: *Keys to Winning Bridge*
1, 2	Truscott, D.: *Bid Better, Play Better*
1, 2	Truscott, D.: *Winning Declarer Play*
2, 3	Watson: *Play of the Hand*
3	Woolsey: *Matchpoints*
3	Woolsey: *Partnership Defense*

NOTE: You cannot go wrong with any book by Larry Cohen, Audrey Grant, Eddie Kantar, Mike Lawrence, Barbara Seagram or Frank Stewart... The above books have been in my library for many years and I have learned much from them.

TWENTY

Play Online and Use Computer Programs To Improve

"'Tis not knowing much but what is useful that makes a wise man."

−Dr. Thomas Fuller

IN THE "GOOD OLD DAYS" when I learned to play bridge, if you wanted to become a better player, the options were limited. You could play, take lessons or read books (at least there were plenty of classics available; in college, we would pour over the world championship books and try to bid slams as well as the legendary Blue Team or the Aces).

It's a different story today. It's only a question of how much time you want to devote to becoming better and to avoid being fired from your job or thrown out of your family.

Following are a few possibilities that you can check out at baronbarclay.com or other sources:

1. The most popular bridge program for many years has been the Bridge Baron. Although I've had countless people approach me, assuming I produced it, I've had to tell them I wasn't involved. The program could have been called the Bridge King, Queen, Duke or Duchess just as easily. I'm glad it's a highly rated program so I don't have to apologize for having my name on it. A tremendous advantage the Baron has is being available on a CD or for download. It's also updated frequently, usually annually.

2. Jack is another well-respected computer program that is available on a CD or for download.

3. There are many other excellent programs from some of the top authors and teachers such as Larry Cohen, Audrey Grant, Eddie Kantar, Mike Lawrence and many others. These are available on a CD that you can load into your computer.

4. GOTO Bridge is the latest software for Windows with unlimited deals and feedback for each hand (Windows only).

5. Vu-Bridge quizzes can be loaded on your computer, tablet or phone. There are plenty of hands for beginning and intermediate players.

6. Bridge Base Online is a hugely popular website on which you can compete against players all over the world. It's the largest bridge site anywhere and it's free. You can practice with your partner and teammates or play in a duplicate game. Developed by Fred Gitelman, it has been enormously helpful in teaching new players and helping everyone to improve.

7. A site I enjoy frequently is Bridge Winners. There are brilliant articles by many of the game's best, countless quizzes, videos, polls, tournament reports and convenient tools to help you improve. Gavin Wolpert, Jason Feldman and Steve Weinstein are the brains behind this impressive website.

TWENTY-ONE

The More Experienced Partner Should Adapt to Changes in Your System

BY KEITH HANSON

"Always keep an open mind and a compassion-ate heart."

—Phil Jackson

IT'S MORE IMPORTANT to be comfortable with your methods than what you agree to play. When you are the more experienced player, the following are my recommendations:

1. Play a basic system that your partner is familiar with, so he will feel more at ease. He will probably be nervous and intimidated enough without having more to worry about than he already faces. He is going to feel under pressure to perform at his best to impress you and the last thing either of you needs is his brain swirling around, unsure of his system.

2. Use leads and signals that are what your partner normally plays. This will make him more comfortable and allow him to play in tempo, as well as make the best play more often.
3. Avoid any bid that might confuse your partner.
4. Make sure you are pleasant and friendly (like you should naturally be, no matter who you play with).
5. If you have a poor result, mark it on your convention card and discuss it after the round. The only topics you should bring up during the round are those to clarify your system, so you don't have a misunderstanding during the rest of the round (This is another principle that is always a good plan).

KEITH HANSON of Boca Raton, Florida is one of the most popular teachers in the country. A graduate of the University of Iowa, Keith is a lifelong St. Louis Cardinal fan. Along with an impressive tournament record, he is the best-selling author of "Winning Bridge Intangibles" with Mike Lawrence, "Card Play Fundamentals" with Easley Blackwood, "Fingertip Bridge" and "The Art of Bidding."

RANDY: Keith and I had an enjoyable association when I edited and published his first two books for Devyn Press, named after my daughter.

♠ ♡ ◇ ♣

TWENTY-TWO

Always Try to Make Life Easy For Your Partner

BY MARK YAEGER

"Try not. Do or do not, there is no try."

–Yoda, The Empire Strikes Back

AS WE HAVE DISCUSSED previously in great detail, the most important trait to be a winning player is to be a good partner and teammate. This is absolutely true in every game, sport, marriage, the business world and everywhere in the world.

As Warren Buffett explains, "You can be the world's greatest bridge player, but someone else is going to be sitting across the table from you. If you behave in a way, any way, that inhibits that person from playing up to his or her potential, you are not going to get as good a result as you would if you knew how to work with other human beings. It's terribly important."

The most telling compliment when players, coaches and sportswriters were talking about the basketball legends Larry Bird and Magic Johnson: They always made the other players around them better. They simply made it easier for teammates by thinking of the team first, positioning themselves in the best place on the floor, passing brilliantly and taking advantage of each player's strengths.

Bridge is similar. You will have many chances to avoid putting partner in an uncomfortable position during the bidding and play of the hand. Try to guide him through the auction without making bids that are unfamiliar to him. Anticipate any problems that might occur in future rounds of bidding. Don't make a bid that you haven't discussed in detail. Make sure partner will understand whether a bid is forcing or non-forcing. A good partnership attempts to minimize the number of bids and auctions that create uncertainty.

Sometimes you can take control of the defense when it's unclear to partner how to proceed. You can also avoid making life difficult for him at the end of a hand by not squeezing or pseudo-squeezing him when he is ready to claim the rest.

Similarly, one of your important roles when defending is to put yourself in partner's place. Keep your plays as simple as possible and make signals that give your partnership the best chance to cash all of the tricks you are entitled to take. Talk about your signaling methods, so you are both comfortable with what you are playing. Like playing too many conventions, using very sophisticated signals when one or both of you doesn't understand them completely doesn't make sense.

Always consider what your partner needs to know during the play, even if it's crystal clear to you. Try to send him that information.

To continue the theme we've stressed throughout this book, part of making life easy for partner is to sympathize when he has made an error, regardless of how costly or ridiculous.

I'll share a hand from Frank Stewart's daily column (if he's not in your newspaper, you can find it at baronbarclay.com).

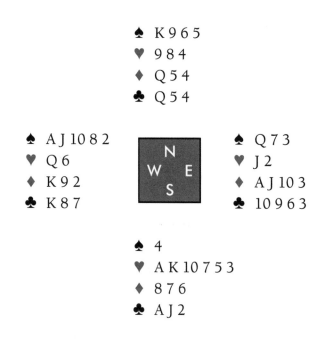

♠ K 9 6 5
♥ 9 8 4
♦ Q 5 4
♣ Q 5 4

♠ A J 10 8 2   ♠ Q 7 3
♥ Q 6   ♥ J 2
♦ K 9 2   ♦ A J 10 3
♣ K 8 7   ♣ 10 9 6 3

♠ 4
♥ A K 10 7 5 3
♦ 8 7 6
♣ A J 2

WEST	NORTH	EAST	SOUTH
1♠	Pass	2♠	3♥
All Pass			

This is an example of when East could make life much easier for partner. After the opening lead of the ♠A, East played the 3, because he didn't like spades. West was unsure how to continue, so he led another spade at trick two. After pitching a diamond on the King, declarer made three, losing one spade, two diamonds and a club.

Notice the difference if East plays the ♠Q at trick one. This highest spade shows partner that he has cards in the higher-ranking suit, diamonds. After the defense cashes three diamonds, they have five tricks to defeat 3♥.

Here is a problem that not every defender would solve correctly:

DEALER: North • VULNERABLE: Both

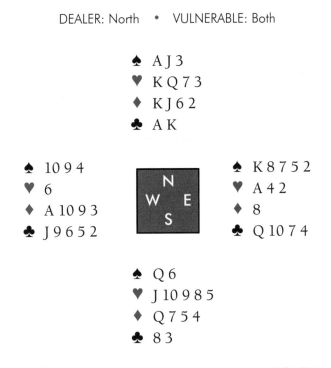

♠ A J 3
♥ K Q 7 3
♦ K J 6 2
♣ A K

♠ 10 9 4
♥ 6
♦ A 10 9 3
♣ J 9 6 5 2

♠ K 8 7 5 2
♥ A 4 2
♦ 8
♣ Q 10 7 4

♠ Q 6
♥ J 10 9 8 5
♦ Q 7 5 4
♣ 8 3

WEST	NORTH	EAST	SOUTH
	2NT	Pass	3♥
Pass	4♣	Pass	4♥
All pass			

West led the ♠10, the 3 was played from dummy, and East won the king. He now returned the ♦8. West knew his partner had to possess the ace of trumps to defeat the contract. Unsure whether East had a singleton or doubleton diamond, he ducked and the contract succeeded.

East's correct play is simple. He should cash his ♥A before leading his singleton diamond. Now his partner has no choice except the winning play.

Here is another example of helping partner:

The following deal (the cards are changed slightly for illustrative purposes) was played by Eric Murray in the 1980 Team Olympiad. This deal illustrates these concepts:

1. Form a picture of all 52 cards when you are defending, not only the 26 you can see.
2. Holdings that seem insignificant at the time can play a vital role in the defense.
3. Help partner whenever possible.

The opponents arrive at 7NT. South has opened a strong NT and denied a four-card major. North has shown a five-card heart suit.

Opening lead: ♠9

♠ K Q 5
♥ K Q 7 3 2
♦ A Q 4
♣ K 2

♠ 9 8 3 2
♥ J 10 9 8
♦ 6 5 2
♣ 10 7

You see dummy and what do you know? The declarer has at least seven cards in the minors and only your partner can stop him from taking four tricks in one of those suits. With seven winners in the minors, he will make his contract.

You have one piece of crucial information, that partner doesn't need to protect diamonds. Why? If partner has four or more diamonds, declarer has 3 or fewer, so the suit isn't a threat. When declarer cashes his top hearts, you play the J-10-9 in that order. This screams to partner that you have diamonds under control (the higher-ranking of the two relevant suits), so he must retain his clubs.

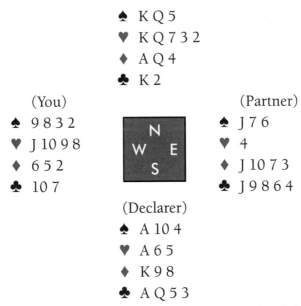

♠ K Q 5
♥ K Q 7 3 2
♦ A Q 4
♣ K 2

(You)
♠ 9 8 3 2
♥ J 10 9 8
♦ 6 5 2
♣ 10 7

(Partner)
♠ J 7 6
♥ 4
♦ J 10 7 3
♣ J 9 8 6 4

(Declarer)
♠ A 10 4
♥ A 6 5
♦ K 9 8
♣ A Q 5 3

At this table Murray made 7NT because the defenders were playing "cards" while you were playing "bridge." You were able to give partner the signal he needed to defeat the contract. This truly is a partnership game.

MARK YAEGER of Hollywood, Florida is a leading American player who has won two National championships, as well as numerous Regionals.

He shared the following story: The Friday night Swiss team game in Miami Beach was my favorite event. I was just a raw player but such greats as the Seamon family, Russ Arnold, Bobby Levin, etc., were there regularly. And, of course, Her Majesty, the fabulous Edith Kemp, whom Russ aptly named "The Queen Bee" was present. Fierce, quick and with a nose to sniff out anything that came her way. My favorite deal, ever, was against her.

I was in a small major-suit slam. Edith cashed an ace, leaned back in her chair for a moment to think. She then leaned forward and looked at me. She placed the ♣2 on the table and said to me, "Son, I'm breaking up the squeeze."

I was never so scared in my life at the table. She asked me if she was correct. "Uh, here Miss Queen Bee. You know better than I do. Take a look." "Yep, I'm right. Down one!" And the best thing about her was how gracious she was.

RANDY: Mark was one of my fraternity brothers who learned bridge with me. I frequently drove 75 miles to Jacksonville with him to play in a club game during our senior year (guess that doesn't say much for our social life). We combed through old world championship books together to try to learn slam bidding like the best players in the world. He was my first partner in Gainesville, Florida at the Student Union and we also attended our first Sectional together in Tallahassee. We won a non-masters event and it was as big a thrill as I've ever had in bridge. He has the perfect combination of imagination and humor at the table, along with a unique flair that makes every deal a magnificent adventure.

♠ ♡ ◇ ♣

TWENTY-THREE

Play Against Good Players As Often As Possible

"Twenty years from now you will be more disappointed by the things you didn't do than by the ones you did do. So throw off the bowlines. Sail away from the safe harbor. Catch the trade winds in your sails. Explore. Dream. Discover."

—Mark Twain

WHEN I FIRST STARTED PLAYING in college many years ago, there weren't all the levels of stratified events that are prevalent today. Most of the time, we were learning the game in the same field as many of the top players of that era. Of course, it's an amazing feeling to do well and increase your masterpoint total. However, if you want to improve, one of the best ways is to compete against the best in your area. Sometimes this isn't easy to do, because the events are limited by the number of points you have. But when you have the chance, enter the open game instead of the limited one at your club or in a tournament. Sure, you'll learn some humility (which is a perfect way to keep your ego in check) and you'll improve if you study and work on building a solid partnership.

If you're reluctant to play in the open game or in a stratified event against more experienced players than usual, one of the better players at your club may be willing to assist you. Some clubs have mentoring programs that provide the exciting opportunity to sit across from someone who can help you learn. When you enter an event with better players than you normally compete against, it's also an opportunity to observe how they act, learn some of their tricks of the trade, play against unfamiliar conventions, and evaluate your game.

I'm completely convinced that when I first started playing at the University of Florida Student Union (Go Gators!), I was helped immensely by competing against a number of accomplished players. At least ten of them eventually became world-class experts, so besides my initial passion for the game, we had to improve or risk being embarrassed consistently.

♠ ♡ ◇ ♣

TWENTY-FOUR

Stay in Shape By Finding Activities That Give You More Stamina

"Each of you is perfect as you are. And you all could use a little bit of improvement."

–Shunryu Suzuki

ALTHOUGH IT MIGHT SURPRISE YOU, many of the best bridge players in the world spend much of their spare time improving their physical and mental capabilities away from the table. They schedule time at the gym regularly or have a normal routine of walking, jogging or running. No matter your age or what level player you are, the benefits can be tremendous. And research has shown that meditation, yoga, tai chi and other similar activities improve every part of your life. I learned to meditate almost 50 years ago and it's as important to my well-being as eating and sleeping. I practice it twice daily; I have found that having some quiet time by myself away from all the distractions of life is priceless. Choose activities that stimulate you, because everyone has a different perspective on what is fun (or at least tolerable).

To undermine the positive activities that make you stronger mentally and physically, not surprisingly, there are a number of behaviors that can take their toll on your body:

- Staying up until all hours of the night partying.
- Not getting enough sleep.
- Drinking too much and/or doing drugs.
- Eating a large meal between sessions of an event or just before you are going to play at the club or tournament.
- Gulping down energy drinks. You may feel energized for awhile, but then you come down.

It doesn't take a brain surgeon or prize-winning scientist to explain how exercise and a healthy lifestyle help you win at bridge and in the game of life.

♠ ♡ ◇ ♣

TWENTY-FIVE

Concentrate to the Best of Your Ability at All Times

"A bridge expert can be described in simple terms as a player who makes fewer mistakes than most."

–H.W. Kelsey

CONCENTRATION AT THE TABLE is the number one ingredient to playing well. Although many qualities are important for success at bridge such as technical knowledge, good card sense, excellent judgment, stamina and being a good partner, none of them is more important than concentration. The biggest difference between an expert and a very good player, or a good player and an average one is concentrating to minimize avoidable errors.

It's only natural to make a few mistakes during a session of bridge. There are going to be bids and plays when you aren't perfect or you do something really silly. And there will be times when your judgment is off, you make a wrong guess, you have a bidding misunderstanding, or you didn't know the best bid or play. That's going to happen on some deals, so you cannot afford to lose concentration to make it even harder to achieve a high level of accomplishment.

Much of your success at bridge depends on your ability to keep your mind on the game. Besides technical knowledge, the difference between the expert and you is how the expert keeps his avoidable errors to a minimum, because he has learned to concentrate very well. If you can play up to your capabilities by limiting your lapses in concentration, you will win more often in the long run.

What can you do to improve this crucial part of the game?

1. Save your mental energy by relaxing as much as possible between hands.
2. When you are dummy, try to allow your mind to rest. Follow the play so you can help partner when necessary, but don't analyze the hand in depth.
3. Don't spend a lot of energy on easy hands.
4. Don't spend time and energy trying to solve a problem when it's really a complete guess.
5. Get in the habit of being at your best in competitions that are important to you.
6. Be alert by taking care of yourself (Discussed in detail in Principle #24).
7. Avoid playing too quickly or not thinking through the situation.
8. Try to pay attention to all discards and signals.
9. Count as much as your ability allows.

Some days are simply bad-hair days. Your brain won't be in high gear (personal issues, medication, aging, etc.). On those days, you'll make errors, so just do the best you can and accept it.

In his classic book, "Improve Your Bridge", H.W. Kelsey shares how his teammate Victor Goldberg would treat lapses with proper sympathy. Victor would ask, "What happened on Board 31?" And without any hostility he would comment, "A cow flew by, did it?" Hopefully, you and your partner will concentrate, so few cows will fly by when you are playing.

♠ ♡ ◇ ♣

TWENTY-SIX

Remember That at Matchpoints a Terrible Board Is Only a Zero

"Losing isn't always the end; sometimes it becomes the beginning."

–Joseph Duffy

ALTHOUGH IT'S IMPORTANT to be a steady and consistent player, duplicate bridge allows you to make each session a thrilling adventure if it suits your personality. I really enjoy playing matchpoints, because it gives me ample opportunities to go out on a limb, take chances and make as many dangerous or crazy bids as my partnership can tolerate. The luxury built into duplicate bridge is that no matter how hopeless your result, it's only one board. If you go down 1700 against a partscore, it's no worse than allowing the opponents to make an impossible overtrick or game…and the best news is you can earn the matchpoints back on the very next board, maybe even against the same opponents.

The best duplicate player of all time, Barry Crane, understood this as well as anyone. There have been numerous successful pairs over the years who won by solid, expert play; their technique and partnership cooperation were enough to win them many events. However, there are many top experts, like Crane, who take their matchpoint life in their hands board after board. They pile up winning scores because they know that most of the time their tactics will work; they suffer a bad board occasionally, but they earn more tops than bottoms, so that strategy wins in the long run. If you earn a top on ⅔ of the boards and a bottom on ⅓ of the boards, you'll have almost 67%, which will win almost every session.

Some top pairs have a "pitcher" and a "catcher", with the pitcher taking risky chances in the bidding, while the catcher is generally more conservative in his approach. This allows his partner more latitude to make more aggressive preempts and competitive bids. It's important for each player to understand his role in the partnership. Have this discussion in your partnerships so that both of you are on the same page when it comes to duplicate strategy.

TWENTY-SEVEN

Smart Players Try For the Best Result Possible, Not the Best Possible Result

"So it's not the handling of difficult hands that makes the winning player. There aren't enough of them. It's the ability to avoid messing up the easy ones."

—S.J. Simon

THIS IS PROFOUND ADVICE from Mr. Simon in his classic book, "Why You Lose at Bridge." Even though it was published in 1946 over 70 years ago, it has been voted the #1 bridge book ever written in several prominent polls. I published and edited over 200 books at Baron Barclay and I was as excited about having the rights to "Why You Lose" and another classic by him, "Cut for Partners", as any books I ever produced.

What S.J. means by the above advice is to try to achieve a reasonable result on each hand, based on who is sitting across the table from you. You should limit your ambition to this goal. The less accomplished your partner is, the more you should stick to this principle. Please just accept your disasters calmly and cheerfully when they happen and do the best you can. As a wise philosopher once explained, "Sometimes you are the pigeon and sometimes you are the statue."

The experienced player, someone who wins consistently, understands this concept. This is a dilemma many of the top bridge professionals face when they are playing with clients. This is also the situation when a very good club or tournament player partners with someone whose ability isn't at the same level as his. If they are smart, they play practical bridge. They realize that there are weaknesses in partner's game and they take this into account during the game. He is the opposite of Simon's character, the Unlucky Expert, who loses his shirt because he tries for the best possible result instead of the best result possible. A subtle but significant difference.

It doesn't make sense to bid to an iffy contract if partner doesn't have the expertise to make it. If he is going to be the declarer, it makes sense to be conservative during the auction. If you are slated to be the declarer, it's a different story because you'll make the contract most of the time.

Understand that you are playing with a partner who lacks your ability, so relax and enjoy the session. Another important point that is consistent with being a good partner: Realize how nervous and intimated your partner is when playing with you. Go out of your way to make them feel confident and happy to spend the session with you. And if you are the inexperienced player in the partnership, learn what you can and be easy on yourself.

S.J. SIMON (1904–1948) whose nickname was Skid, was a novelist and bridge writer. He was one of the top players in the world in his heyday and one of the best-loved British bridge personalities. In the years preceding World War II, he was the winner or finalist in every major English competition. Simon was one of the creators of the popular ACOL System, as well as writing very popular humorous novels.

Your System, Conventions, and Strategy

♤ ♡ ◇ ♧

TWENTY-EIGHT

The System You Play Is Not Nearly As Important As How Well You Play the System

"Embrace simplicity. Have few desires."

–Lao Tzu

ALTHOUGH I HAVE enjoyed playing the Precision Club since I started my bridge education in the early 70s, most of the time whatever convention card I play is OK with me. I have played with many competent people, and if we hadn't played previously, we used a very simple card.

There are countless stories of new or almost new pairs winning major events. The common thread in these victories was that the winners usually kept their systems relatively easy to understand and remember. Most of their success came from bidding accurately, playing the cards well as declarers, taking their tricks on defense and seldom losing their concentration.

The bottom line is that you should worry less about expanding your bidding system and spend more time improving your basic skills.

I've had surprisingly good results with unfamiliar partners. I try to pay close attention to every card to avoid embarrassing myself and to (I hope) fool my partner into thinking I know what I'm doing. There is, of course, the added benefit of having a minimum of misunderstandings. Your brain isn't constantly having to worry about the meaning of an obscure bid or whether the last call was forcing.

When you play with your regular partner, try to use the same convention card as often as possible, so that you are both completely comfortable with your system. When you want to add something new, just be sure to add a little at a time and discuss it thoroughly.

♠ ♡ ◇ ♣

TWENTY-NINE

Arrive Early To Discuss Your System with Partner

"The best bid in the world isn't worth a thing if partner doesn't know what it means."

–Bill Root

IT'S A SIMPLE CONCEPT, but one that many players ignore at their peril. Unless there is a good reason to rush into the playing area at game time, you should give yourself and your partner a reasonable amount of time to get comfortable and talk about your methods. Even if you are an experienced pair, it makes sense to discuss a few items on your convention card or ask questions about specific conventions you play. This is much like arriving at the golf course or tennis court to hit balls before you play. Although in physical sports it is really essential, in a mental sport like bridge, it also makes sense.

It's also helpful to make sure your convention card is 100% accurate, especially if you change what you play sometimes or if you play with more than one partner.

It's even better if you have your entire system written down, but most of us don't have time or the inclination to do this. Whatever level player you are, it's certainly worthwhile if you tackle your bidding system in detail. I have found it is surprising how many sequences and conventions can be misunderstood or forgotten, even if you are an experienced partnership. For example, one of my regular partners (we have played for years) and I didn't realize that we had different cue bidding tendencies (I was cue bidding first- or second-round control, while he cue bid only aces or voids). There are many concepts to discuss and it's easy to miss some of them even if you play together frequently.

♠ ♡ ◇ ♣

THIRTY

Consent to Play Only Conventions With Which You Are Totally Comfortable

"Once somebody called me the Simple Simon of bridge." I said, "Thank you very much. I appreciate the compliment."

–Charles Goren

S TAYMAN AND BLACKWOOD are the only conventions that are absolutely necessary for most players (I'll add Jacoby Transfers and Negative Doubles close behind). The important point is that if you place a new convention on your card, make sure you understand it and you have discussed it at length with your partner. Many players think it makes them look "cool" or experienced to have all the new bids on their cards. Sure, many of the top players use complex bidding systems, but they study and practice constantly. If you don't play often or have various partners, KISS (Keep It Simple, Stupid).

I recently played against two students who had just finished a few beginner lessons and afterwards decided to try the open game at our local club. Surprisingly, this pair had numerous advanced conventions that even experienced players rarely play, such as upside-down signals and a complicated version of Blackwood. As they demonstrated during the boards they played against us, they hadn't yet learned the basics. Instead of discussing the fundamentals and focusing on standard bidding, declarer play and defense, they wanted to show everyone all the new conventions they had found to put on their convention card. It's not quite the best way to proceed in their budding bridge careers.

Besides the four conventions I have mentioned as being somewhat essential, here is a list of others that should prove worthwhile once you reach a level at which you feel comfortable with a simple Standard American system:

- A proven method for competing when opponents open 1NT (15–17)
- A more advanced version of Blackwood
- Fourth-suit forcing (Checkback)
- Inverted Minor raises
- Jacoby 2NT
- Lebensohl after your 1NT opening when opponents compete
- Michaels and Unusual 2NT
- New-minor forcing (Checkback)
- Ogust Responses to Weak Two-Bids (or 2NT to ask for a feature)
- Splinter raises
- Two over One Game Force (I'm a huge proponent: it makes life easy)

One of the conventions that I've never liked at all is Drury (and all the various forms of it). I feel it's better to use common sense and judgment as the bidding proceeds after you or your partner open in third seat; I've never found this popular convention helpful or necessary, although there are many good players who swear by it.

The most important question your partnership should answer when deciding which conventions to add to your system is how much time you are going to spend discussing them. Make sure you go over the details when you decide to add a new wrinkle to your card. It is really helpful if you actually write each convention down with all of the variations and possibilities. This is especially important if you frequently play with different partners. It's not a bad idea to agree to play the same convention card with everyone if you have several partnerships.

Here are a few of the best books on conventions to add to your library of learning:

- *25 Bridge Conventions You Should Know* by Barbara Seagram & Marc Smith
- *25 More Bridge Conventions You Should Know* by Barbara Seagram & David Bird
- *57+ Bridge Conventions Made Easy* by Alvin Lesser
- *ACBL: Commonly Used Conventions in the 21st Century*
- *Bridge Basics 3: Popular Conventions* by Audrey Grant
- *Bridge Conventions in Depth* by Pam & Matt Granovetter
- Modern Bridge Conventions by Bill Root & Richard Pavlicek

♠ ♡ ◇ ♣

THIRTY-ONE

Use the 80-20 Rule When Creating a Bidding System

BY RALPH LETIZIA

"Common sense is seeing things as they are and doing things as they ought to be."

–Harriet Beecher Stowe

THERE ARE MANY PLAYERS, especially experts, who have a very comprehensive bidding system spanning dozens, or even hundreds of pages. They depend on these notes to ensure that virtually every situation is covered. It makes sense, because, like professional athletes, they are competing against the world's best and, for some of them, it is their livelihood.

Unless you are one of these gifted champions, even though you strive to win as much as possible, your goals are more modest. So it makes sense for your partnership to use the 80-20% rule; that is, to focus on the 20% of your system that occurs 80% of the time. Think about it: there are many bids and sequences that have never or very seldom come up in your auctions. Much of the work of preparing your system is wasted time. Why not make sure you understand the bids that appear consistently?

These obvious areas of focus include:

- How solid your opening bids and overcalls should be
- Opening NT sequences
- Major-suit raises
- 1NT Forcing
- Requirements for various kinds of doubles
- Competitive bidding sequences (because it is rare these days to have a free run in the auction).
- Slam and cue bidding structure
- Preemptive style

These are just a few of the most important topics to discuss in detail. It's a good idea to spend time going over the convention card and writing down your preferences together. Then you each have a basic structure of your agreements and you can add changes in the future.

RALPH LETIZIA of Louisville, Kentucky is a Cyber Security Professional, huge sports fan and rescues Brittany Spaniels. He is a two-time National champion and one of the Midwest's top players. Ralph is a tireless advocate of improving ethics in our game; he has devoted much of his time to the Conduct and Ethics committees, often serving as chairman.

RANDY: Ralph is my most frequent and most trusted partner. We've never had a cross word at the bridge table, and we always have fun, even when we have no clue what we are doing.

THIRTY-TWO

Learn the Rule of 20 for When To Open the Bidding

"I favor light opening bids. When you're my age, you're never sure they're going to get back to you in time."

—Oswald Jacoby at the age of 77

REGARDLESS OF WHAT METHOD you use to evaluate hands, the Rule of 20 has proven to be very effective on a vast majority of deals. It is generally applied only in first or second seat when you are deciding whether to open the bidding on the one level.

It's simple: Add the number of cards in your two longest suits + your high card points; if the total is 20 or more, open...if not, pass (or occasionally preempt). I have found this works well for me, eliminating much of the guesswork on whether to open. It also allows me to open distributional hands, so I don't have to apologize to my partner, who knows I am using the Rule of 20. For example, if I'm 6-6 and have 8 HCP, it's an easy hand to open. (I must admit that when I'm 4-4 with 11 HCP sometimes I fib a little and open anyway when I'm playing with a partner who approves).

Some advocates of the similar Rule of 22 use the same guidelines and add another stipulation: You also must have two quick tricks (two aces, one ace and two kings, or four kings). This doesn't suit my style, because I prefer opening as many hands as possible. However, if you would rather adapt this version, that's perfectly all right.

Here are some quizzes:

1.   ♠ A 7 5 4
     ♥ Q J 7
     ♦ VOID
     ♣ Q J 10 9 5 2

2.   ♠ K J 3
     ♥ A J 9 8 7 4 3
     ♦ 10
     ♣ 7 6

3.   ♠ Q 10 2
     ♥ 6 4
     ♦ K 10 5 3
     ♣ A Q 7 2

4.   ♠ A J 10 7 3
     ♥ A J 8 6 3
     ♦ 6 4
     ♣ 5

5.   ♠ A J 10 7 5 4
     ♥ Q 8 6 3
     ♦ Q 9
     ♣ 9

6.   ♠ A
     ♥ K 8 3 2
     ♦ Q 6 5
     ♣ Q 10 9 3 2

7.   ♠ Q 10 5 4
     ♥ A 10 8 7 6 2
     ♦ K 9
     ♣ 4

8.   ♠ J 10 8 6 5
     ♥ K Q 7 3
     ♦ 6
     ♣ A J 2

9. ♠ 7
    ♥ 4 2
    ♦ A Q 9 7 4 3
    ♣ K J 8 6

SOLUTIONS TO QUIZZES

1. Using the Rule of 20, this is an automatic 1♣ opening. It's a reasonable playing hand, so you have nothing to be ashamed of. For those of you who prefer the Rule of 22, a timid pass is the bid.

2. With only 9 HCP and 10 cards in your two longest suits, according to the Rule 20, this is a pass or 3♥ opening. My preference is to open 1♥, rebid the suit as the auction develops, and apologize to partner if it doesn't work out. I'm playing with a sympathetic partner, so I can do this without causing a major problem. That's one of the reasons it's so important to play with someone you like and get along with: You can use your judgment when you feel it's best.

3. 11 HCP + 8 cards in my two longest suits. So the Rule says to pass. This is the example I mention above when I'll probably fib and open 1♦, especially not vulnerable. It's certainly OK to pass; it all depends on your personality, style and partnership agreement.

4. A perfect 1♠ opening with easy rebids. You even have your two quick tricks if you use the Rule of 22.

5. Again, a point short, but a good playing hand. Go ahead and open 1♠ if you are comfortable in doing so.

6. Twenty on the nose, so a perfectly good 1♣ opening.
7. Like number 5, only 19, so do what your heart tells you is best.
8. Open unless you use the Rule of 22.
9. Similar to number 8. You have easy rebids.

♤ ♡ ◇ ♧

THIRTY-THREE

Use the Rule of 15 When Deciding Whether To Open In Fourth Seat

"Next to sound judgment, diamonds and pearls are the rarest things in the world."

—Jean de la Bruyere

A NOTHER SIMPLE RULE, but also effective. Add your HCP to the number of spades you hold...if the total is 15 or more, open. If not, pass the deal out. It's not always perfect, but it makes sense. The spade suit frequently controls the auction when the points are split somewhat equally around the table. A corollary to the rule is to look around the table. The better the opponents, the more it makes sense to pass out the hand and go on to the next one (when you have a close decision). You should also consider the state of the match in a team game or if you think you need a top playing matchpoints.

Here are a few examples:

1. ♠ A J 9 7 6
   ♥ K 7
   ♦ Q 8 6
   ♣ 7 5 2
   10 HCP + 5 spades = 15 so open 1♠

2. ♠ 9 6
   ♥ A K Q 8 7
   ♦ K 8 5 4 3
   ♣ 5
   12 HCP (but a great playing hand) + 2 spades = only 14, but open anyway

3. ♠ J
   ♥ K J 6 4
   ♦ A 9 6 5
   ♣ K 8 7 4
   12 HCP + 1 spade = 13 Pass

4. ♠ K 6 5
   ♥ A J 8 7 3
   ♦ 8 5 4
   ♣ K 7
   11 HCP + 3 spades = 14 Pass (but if you want to open, it's OK)

THIRTY-FOUR

After Partner Has Passed In First or Second Seat, Be Aggressive

"It is well known that in third seat you must have 13 cards to open the bidding."

–Edgar Kaplan

WHEN YOU ARE in third seat and the bidding has gone: Pass, Pass...all options are open to you. There are many good reasons to open the bidding light or to make a disruptive preempt. If you have a normal opening bid, there is a decent chance that you have the balance of points in the deck and you can make your usual bid to see how the bidding proceeds.

However, if you have fewer points than a normal opener, it's an entirely different situation. Now the opponents have most of the assets and it's crucial to make life as difficult as possible for them. No matter how weak your hand is there are various actions to avoid having your opponents reach their optimum contract easily. As Larry Cohen's longtime partner Marty Bergen showed him, "Bidding when you are the third seat opener isn't bridge."

There are four actions you can take in third seat when the bidding hasn't been opened yet:

1. A bid at the one level
2. A strong opening bid such as 2♣ or 2NT
3. A weak preemptive bid
4. Pass

My advice is to open at the one level whenever it is logical to do so. The question is: how light do you open when you don't possess a full opener? The proper answer depends on several factors: if you have a logical bid, if you have a reasonable rebid, the vulnerability, and the personality and tendencies of your partnership.

When you have a full opening bid, you should take your normal action in third or fourth seat, just like you had opened in first or second chair. However, when you have less than your usual opening, there are a number of good reasons to bid anyway:

1. You may help your partner find the best opening lead.
2. You may help your partner avoid a disastrous opening lead.
3. You may still have a good fit and be able to make a partscore or even game.
4. You may be able to steal the auction from the opponents when they have an awkward holding, they are reluctant to make a dangerous bid, or the high cards are divided equally between them.

5. You may have a profitable sacrifice available.
6. The opponents may bid too high.
7. Your bid might push them to the wrong contract.
8. Whatever the opponents hold, in a vast majority of deals when you open the auction, it makes reaching the best contract more difficult.

Another thought about third-seat openers: Many players love to play the Drury convention, so responder can tell partner he has more than a simple raise (Drury is used only with major-suit openers. In its original form, a conventional 2♣ response by a passed hand asks opener to clarify his strength. Many pairs currently use a modified form of the convention). As I have previously expressed, I have never liked Drury or played it, but you can certainly use it.

Let's test your third-hand bidding with a few quizzes (let's assume neither side is vulnerable):

1. ♠ K J 9 5 4
    ♥ K 9
    ♦ K 8 7 2
    ♣ 7 6

2. ♠ A 3
    ♥ 10 8 7 4
    ♦ Q 8
    ♣ A 10 9 6 5

3. ♠ A J 7 6
    ♥ 8
    ♦ K Q 9 5 3
    ♣ 7 6 5

4. ♠ K Q 9 5 3
    ♥ 7
    ♦ A J 10 3
    ♣ 6 4 3

5. ♠ K J 10 8   6. ♠ A Q J 7
    ♥ 8 6 4 3   ♥ 8 6 4
    ♦ 7 4 2   ♦ A Q
    ♣ A K   ♣ J 10 9 5

ANSWERS TO QUIZ:

1. Even though you only have 10 HCP, you should open the bidding 1♠. This is an easy third-seat opening bid. You have the spade suit and you can probably outbid the opponents for a plus score or small minus if partner can support your suit.
2. Open the bidding 1♣ to tell partner to lead a club. Your partner may be able to compete.
3. The best opening bid is 1♦ in 3rd seat. You have close to a normal opening bid, so get into the auction and hope it's your hand.
4. Open 1♠ and on a good day, your partner will raise your spades or bid 2♦. If he bids, 1NT or 2♣, your best bid is 2♦.
5. 1♠. Maybe you will win the auction, but if the opponents outbid you, a spade lead should be helpful.
6. Open 1♣, just like you would in first or second seat with your solid opening bid.

$\spadesuit \heartsuit \diamondsuit \clubsuit$

THIRTY-FIVE

Don't Be a Slave to the Point Count

"The truth is rarely pure and never simple."

—Oscar Wilde

ALTHOUGH ALMOST EVERYONE uses the Work point count introduced by Bryant McCampbell in 1915 and made popular by Milton Work and Charles Goren, it's not perfect. The 4-3-2-1 count is usually close to being accurate, but there are flaws that you should be aware of:

1. Aces and kings are undervalued (some say aces are greatly undervalued). An ace is worth between ½ to 1 extra point, depending on who you ask.
2. Queens and jacks are overvalued.
3. Long suits are undervalued.
4. Balanced hands are overvalued.
5. Tens are valuable and are certainly worth more than zero.
6. Combinations of honors are worth more together than in different suits.

7. Singleton honor cards (K, Q or J) are not worth their usual value. It's a good idea to deduct at least one point when you possess a singleton honor.

8. Quick tricks (A-Q of the same suit= 1½, A or K-Q = 1; K-x = ½) make a hand more valuable.

9. There are other methods of hand evaluation. Most of them were used in the early days of bridge and are now obsolete. An exception is the Losing Trick Count which has been played since the 1930s and is still very popular today. It is only applicable for suit contracts and the strength of a hand is based on the number of expected losers. In its simplest form, the number of losers is determined as follows: With three or more cards, the number of losers in a suit is equal to the number of missing high card honors (the ace, king and queen). For example, A-x-x counts as two losers and K-Q or K-Q-x count as one loser. With a doubleton, the queen is counted as a small card and any singleton (without the ace) is counted as one loser.

THIRTY-SIX

Open a Strong 1NT with a Five-Card Major with 15–17 High Card Points

"A few strong instincts and a few plain rules."

–William Wordsworth

MY RECOMMENDATION is to always open 1NT when you have a balanced hand and a five-card major. When you have five spades or five hearts with 5-3-3-2 distribution and 15–17 HCP, open 1NT. Keep it simple; there are few exceptions to this principle.

If you open 1♥, your partner responds 1♠ and you rebid 1NT, it shows about 12–14 HCP. If you rebid 2NT, it shows about 18–19 HCP. So you can see that if the bidding goes 1♥ by you (with five hearts and 15–17 points) and then 1♠ by partner, you usually have a tough rebid problem. If you open 1♠ (with five spades and 15–17 HCP) and partner responds 1NT (forcing), it's also not easy to find a proper rebid most of the time. That's why opening 1NT in these situations makes sense.

Even if you miss an eight- or nine-card fit in a major because you opened 1NT (15–17), you might still achieve an average or better result. You might receive a helpful opening lead, the deal could be hard to defend, or there might be the same number of tricks available at notrump as in the major. It's true that you could play in an inferior contract by opening 1NT, but in the long run, this is a winning strategy.

How do you tell your partner that you have five of a major when he bids 2♣ (Stayman)? The easiest method is to jump to three of your major to show five hearts or five spades. This will lead to a simple auction because you won't encounter a problem on most hands. The most difficult problem in using this bid is when your partner has a weak hand and intended to pass your response to 2♣. Since he should have reasonable support for your major (at least three), you are a level higher than partner intended, but you have at least an eight card fit. Not a perfect situation, but we've all been in worse.

Another effective option over a 1NT (or 2NT) opener (for more experienced partnerships) is using the Puppet Stayman convention invented by Kit Woolsey. This can be an effective bid because it allows the responder to disclose his distribution instead of the opener, so valuable information is withheld from the opponents. It also enables the opener to show a five-card major if he has one. Over 1NT, 2♣ asks if opener has a five-card major; if not, he bids 2♦. Responder bids the major he doesn't have over 2♦ or 2NT with both majors. Opener can now choose the proper suit or notrump to play in, after giving as little information as possible to the opponents.

Although I like to open 1NT on any balanced hand with a five-card major, not everyone likes this principle. Many authorities tend to open 1NT with five hearts, because there are usually rebid problems as discussed above. With five spades, if you open 1♠ instead of 1NT, there are fewer auctions when you have a difficult or impossible rebid. There are also many top players and authors who use their judgment on whether to open 1NT with a five-card major. They take into account the quality of the major suit (tending to open 1NT more often when the suit is bad) and also flaws in the other suits, such as having a low doubleton or troubling distribution such as a four-card minor.

In his classic book, "Matchpoints," Kit Woolsey recommends using your judgment when deciding whether to open 1NT with a five-card major. If the hand contains various flaws such as the major being of intermediate strength such as K-J-10-5-4, a worthless doubleton, or having 5-4-2-2 distribution (any four-card side suit), many top players will not open 1NT. However, if you ask various experts, you will find there are different opinions, so there is no right or wrong answer. Just make sure you discuss this with your partner, so you both know what to expect when your partnership opens 1NT.

♠ ♡ ◇ ♣

THIRTY-SEVEN

After Your Partner Opens 1NT, Don't Use Stayman When You Have 4-3-3-3 Distribution

"No matter how good you are, it won't help you if you are playing in the wrong contract."

—George Rosenkranz

WHEN YOU HAVE enough points to bid game in this situation, when you are balanced and have no distributional points, it is better to bid 3NT instead of probing for a major-suit fit. It is usually better to try to take nine tricks at notrump instead of 10 at 4♥ or 4♠. On most hands, you will take as many tricks at notrump as you would in your 4-4 major suit fit. You also have the advantage of not telling the opponents much about your hand and taking away bidding room to keep them from entering the auction. Because the opponents tend to lead one of the majors when Stayman is not used, they may also make a favorable lead for your side.

It might not always be the correct contract, but the odds are in your favor and this is a helpful tip to include in your arsenal. This is advice the experts follow and should allow you to reach the best contract more often.

Here are a few examples of hands that illustrate this point after partner opens 1NT:

1. ♠ K 7 5
   ♥ J 10 8 2
   ♦ J 7 5
   ♣ A K 5

Bid 3NT.

2. ♠ K 4 2
   ♥ Q J 8 7
   ♦ Q 4 3
   ♣ J 8 6

Bid 2NT.

3. ♠ A J 7 6
   ♥ Q 6 5
   ♦ J 8 7
   ♣ K 10 7

Bid 3NT.

4. ♠ K 6 4
   ♥ A Q 4 2
   ♦ K Q 9
   ♣ Q 9 7

Bid 4NT (quantitative) to see if your partner can bid 6NT.

♠ ♡ ◇ ♣

THIRTY-EIGHT

Learn Garbage Stayman

"A short saying often contains much wisdom."

—Sophocles

When you bid Stayman (2♣) over partner's 1NT opening, you usually have a hand that's either invitational or good enough for game or slam. There is an exception, which is accurately named "Garbage" Stayman, because your hand is appropriate for the trash can.

When your hand is short in clubs after the 1NT opening, you have the attractive option of bidding 2♣ and then passing opener's next bid. In almost all cases, when you play 2♦, 2♥ or 2♠, you are in a better contract than 1NT.

The perfect hand for this helpful bid is:

♠ 8 7 4 3
♥ 10 6 3 2
♦ 9 8 6 4 3
♣ —

or a similar hand with 4-4-5-0 distribution. However, as long as you have at least three cards in each of the majors, at least four diamonds and no more than a doubleton club, go ahead and bid Stayman. (The exception: If you have a decent five-card major, three of the other major and four diamonds, go ahead and make a normal Jacoby transfer).

Here are a few more example hands when Garbage System should be used:

1. ♠ 8 6 5 4
   ♥ 7 5 4 3 2
   ♦ K 10 7 4
   ♣ —

2. ♠ J 10 6
   ♥ J 9 5 3
   ♦ J 7 5 4 2
   ♣ 7

3. ♠ 10 8 6 2
   ♥ 7 6 4
   ♦ 10 8 6 3
   ♣ K 3

Another possibility once you bid 2♣ is that the opponents will win the auction. Then you can relax and try to defeat them. If your partner bids 2♦, 2♥ or 2♠, you should have a reasonable chance to make it or take a minus score lower than you would receive for defending.

♤ ♡ ◇ ♧

THIRTY-NINE

Playing a Weak No Trump Opening Makes Life Difficult for the Opponents

"When we lose the right to be different, we lose the right to be free."

–Charles Evans Hughes

BECAUSE I HAVE PLAYED the Precision Club most of my bridge life, I've always been comfortable using a weak 1NT opening bid. The range has varied between 11–14 HCP, 13–15 and 10–12 currently (which many of the experts prefer). Here are the reasons why weak 1NTs are so popular:

1. It puts tremendous pressure on the opponents. Very few people like to sit down at a table when you are playing a weak 1NT opener. You are completely (you will be) prepared for any bidding sequences that develop, while the opponents are not used to dealing with your 1NT openers. Their auctions can be awkward and frustrating. Many pairs don't have the best weapons to compete.

2. Balanced minimum hands cause many complications in most systems that use a strong 1NT opening bid. There can be a problem in selecting the best suit to open, as well as rebid issues. Weak 1NTs solve most of these difficulties.

3. When you open 1NT, you have preempted the opponents and they must start any communication on the two level.

4. On many auctions, especially against less-experienced pairs, the opponents are unsure about coming into the auction.

5. There are simple ways to show a strong notrump when you open a weak notrump, so you are really not giving up anything. For example, most Precision pairs who play a 13–15 notrump use a 1♣ opening and a 1NT rebid to show 16–18 HCP.

6. You can play a stronger notrump when you are vulnerable, so your risk of being penalized is lessened. I'm most comfortable (and I think it's the most effective system) with using a 10–12 notrump ONLY not vulnerable in 1st or 2nd seat. In all other seats, we use a 14–16 notrump.

7. Balanced minimums are opened 1NT, so constructive bidding is easier in other auctions.

8. Rebids are simplified and the range is narrow. If we open 1♦ not vulnerable in 1st or 2nd seat, a 1NT rebid shows 13–15, because we would have opened 1NT with 10–12. If we open 1♦ vulnerable in 3rd or 4th seat, a rebid of 1NT shows 11–13, because a 1NT opening would show 14–16. Simple and effective.

9. The weak 1NT bidder's partner is usually well-placed to judge the best action for his side. Weak 1NTs tend to collect more penalties than the strong version.
10. They are fun to play and make me feel like I have an advantage over the strong 1NT bidders.

You can see that there are valid reasons for switching to or at least trying a weak 1NT. As with most conventions and system changes, it's important to have a happy and frequent partnership.

Of course, there are dangers in playing a weak notrump. If it was nearly perfect, almost everyone would use them. The main disadvantages are:

1. You can be doubled without an acceptable escape route and suffer a substantial penalty.

This is true and there are occasions when you will have a negative result. I have found it happens less often than you would expect. Sometimes the opponents bid to take you out of danger. Many opponents don't have the tools to double you, even when they could and should. You can include helpful runouts to help you avoid trouble.

Here are the runouts I use over weak notrumps in all seats:

a. If an opponent doubles, redouble shows a one-suited hand. Opener bids 2♣ and responder passes or bids his suit.

b. If the bidding proceeds, 1NT Double, 2♣ shows clubs and hearts, 2♦ shows diamonds and hearts, 2♥ shows hearts and spades, and 2♠ is natural.

c. If the bidding proceeds, 1NT Double, a pass by responder forces opener to Redouble. Responder then bids 2♣ to show clubs and spades and 2♦ to show diamonds and spades.

d. If the opponents bid, you are off the hook and don't have to bid again.

e. Doubles are for penalty after the opponents bid.

f. If the bidding proceeds, 1NT, pass by your opponent, all bids on the two level are to play (it's usually better to run right away, especially if you have a weak hand) and bids on the three level are invitational.

g. We use 2♣ as non-forcing Stayman (not forcing to game) and 2♦ as forcing Stayman for sequences when we want to reach game.

There are many other refinements and gadgets you can use. I have listed the options that keep the bidding as simple as possible while giving your side an excellent chance to avoid being doubled after you open a weak 1NT.

2. You may miss a 4-4 major suit fit or a good minor-suit fit. This is true; you will suffer occasional bad results. However, there are also hands with 4-4 major-suit fits and minor-suit fits that play just as well or better in notrump.

3. You may go against the field or play the hand from the wrong side. This can also occur, but I have found

that the benefits and drawbacks usually even out in the long run.

4. It can be difficult to know whether to compete or double the opponents when they enter the auction. I have found this to be the most frequent disadvantage. I am aware that it can happen when all four players are guessing what to do after a weak 1NT opener, so we use our best judgment and hope we achieve a reasonable result. Once you decide which point range you will use, here are some usual requirements to open a weak 1NT:

a. 10–12, 11–14, or 13–15 HCP.

b. Balanced distribution (4-3-3-3, 4-4-3-2, 3-3-2-5 or 2-4-2-5 if you have some points in the short suits)

c. No five-card major. (Some weak 1NT pairs open with 5 hearts or 5 spades, but I'd rather open in the major).

d. Two four-card majors are acceptable to me (some pairs don't open 1NT with both of them).

♤ ♡ ◇ ♧

FORTY

Avoid Any Unilateral Decision on the First Round of Bidding

"Gettin' good players is easy. Getting' 'em to play together is the hard part."

–Casey Stengel

RANDY: I learned this sound advice from Gavin Wolpert on his Bridge Winners site. If you haven't been there: bridgewinners.com, you should definitely give it a try. It's free and there are worthwhile articles for every level player. My favorite is a brilliant video by Gavin, detailing how the expert mind works as he shares his thoughts from all 52 final boards from his 2011 NABC Open Pairs win in "Road to Victory" in my hometown of Louisville. His point is that if you make an unusual action on your first bid of the hand, it is usually impossible to show your partner what you really have. If you want to "take a view," wait until later in the bidding to take control or use your impeccable judgment. There are also many other profound comments, showing how a world class player thinks throughout each deal. I learned several new concepts from his video and I'm sure you will also.

GAVIN: Here are a few examples of unilateral decisions that commit the partnership to a specific direction when another option might be better:

1. Bypassing a major suit (even if it's a weak one when your partner has opened 1 of a minor.

   If partner opens 1♣ and you hold:

   > ♠ 10 7 4 3
   > ♥ A J 8
   > ♦ Q 9
   > ♣ Q 9 5 4

   The normal bid is 1♠, hoping you have a 4-4 fit. If you bid 1NT, even though your spades aren't the best, it might play better in an 8-card spade fit instead of NT. By bidding 1♠, you are making the bid that most of the field will choose.

2. Masterminding a hand instead of staying with the field.

   If you hold:

   > ♠ Q 9 8 2
   > ♥ A K J 10
   > ♦ A J 10
   > ♣ 8 5

   and open 1♦ instead of 1NT, you are going against the field who will be opening a strong NT.

3. Making offshape takeout doubles instead of showing discipline. If RHO opens 1♦, with:

a.

♠ A Q 7
♥ A 3
♦ Q 10 6 4
♣ Q 8 7 5

you should probably pass. If you cannot stand passing, 1NT is better than a double. You can find yourself in serious trouble when partner bids hearts. You shouldn't make a takeout double and then bid again unless you have a hand in the 16+ point range.

b.

♠ A Q 6 3
♥ K 9
♦ K 7 5
♣ J 8 6 3

This is another example where you shouldn't make a takeout double after 1♦. If you want to bid, the 4-card spade overcall is less risky than doubling.

4. Making an undisciplined weak two bid or three-level preempt that is outside your partnership agreement (Once partner is a passed hand, then you have more latitude). If you want to use unconventional preempts in first or second seat, you should discuss what is permissible for your partnership.

5. Bidding a 3-card major when your partner has opened the bidding. This can put your partnership in all kinds of trouble from which you cannot escape.

GAVIN WOLPERT lives in Florida with his wife Jenny and their three children. He is one of America's top players and a co-founder of Bridge Winners. Jenny and Gavin met at the 2003 Bermuda Bowl and they travel the world as bridge professionals. He has won National titles with eight different partners, including the Blue Ribbon Pairs with Jenny when they were engaged.

FORTY-ONE

Always Plan Your Second Bid

by Jerry Helms

"By failing to prepare, you are preparing to fail."

—Benjamin Franklin

I 'LL START by giving you timeless advice from Alvin Roth, one of the 20th century's top players and theorists, "Always plan a second bid before you choose a first." This is the best advice I have ever heard about bidding and it is frequently applicable. There are many times when, in isolation, a bid seems reasonable, but when you examine the future possibilities, it's not the best choice.

Here are two useful examples I have discussed in my "Ask Jerry" column in the ACBL Bulletin. In the first I was asked, "What would you do with the following hand?

♠ 8
♥ A Q 10 4
♦ J 9 6 5 3
♣ A J 7

I opened 1♦, partner responded 1♠ and I rebid 1NT despite my singleton spade. We had a poor result on the hand.

JERRY: My advice was to anticipate the likely 1♠ response from partner. A 1NT rebid after opening the bidding should show at least two cards in partner's suit (or at the worst a singleton honor). So one choice is to open 1♥, planning to rebid 2♦ over 1♠; at least I have nine red cards and a two-suited hand. A second option is to open 1♦ and then rebid 2♣ instead of 1NT. At least my partner won't be expecting a balanced hand.

On the second hand, I was asked my opinion about the best opening bid in third seat, both sides vulnerable with:

♠ K
♥ K J 9 4
♦ A 7 5 2
♣ A 10 6 4

I opened 1NT (15–17) and made four. I have seen support for a similar 1NT opening in Bridge World magazine. I was criticized by my opponent for "psyching." What is your opinion?

JERRY: Personally, I think you followed Alvin Roth's advice perfectly; you have a tough bid and your decision made sense. It would have been my only choice, because any other opening bid doesn't show your hand as well as 1NT. Your singleton K of spades is certainly at least as valuable as a small doubleton. In recent years, the ACBL and *Bridge World* have both supported opening 1NT with a singleton A, K, or Q as the best bid with a hand such as yours.

I'll close with an appropriate Jerry-ism:

"The best bid available is often the least bad alternative."

JERRY HELMS has amassed over 25,000 master-points and he has the impressive accomplishment of appearing over 30 consecutive times on the annual Barry Crane Top 500 masterpoint list. Most of his time is spent on group seminars across North America. His unique, humorous style has endeared him to players at all levels and he is well known for his insightful "Jerry-isms," easy tips to remember. Jerry is a featured columnist in the *ACBL Bulletin* and *Better Bridge* magazine and he is a best-selling author of "Helms to HELLO" and "The Best of Ask Jerry," with a new book, "Over My Shoulder" due out soon.

FORTY-TWO

In Every Auction Your Partnership Should Understand Which of You Is the Captain

"There can be only one captain to a ship."

–Thomas John Barnardo

THIS IS AN IMPORTANT CONCEPT, and you should be aware that the captain (the person who decides how high to bid) is not always the player with the stronger hand. The key to remember is that if you have limited your hand to a narrow range, your partner is the captain for the rest of the auction. Strength really has no bearing on who is the captain. It all depends on who limits his hand first.

Sometimes both partners continue to describe their hand during the auction (if neither hand has limited their hand by the first few bids). In this situation, both players can use their judgment and eventually the partnership decides how high to bid.

When you open the bidding 2NT, you have the stronger hand, but your partner knows your point count, so your partner is the captain. When you open 1♠ and your partner limits his hand with a response of 2♠, you are the captain, because your partner has limited his hand.

Let's try some examples:

1. North opens 1NT and South bids to 2♠ to play (or bids 2♥ as a transfer, intending to play in 2♠).
2. North opens the bidding 1♠ and South responds 3♠ (a limit raise, inviting North to bid game).
3. North passes, South opens the bidding 1♥ and North now bids 2♦.
4. North opens the bidding 2♠ (a weak-two bid) and South responds 2NT (asking for a feature or asking North to describe his hand (depending on what 2NT means in your system).
5. North opens the bidding 3♥.
6. North opens the bidding 1♥ and South responds 2♥.
7. North opens the bidding 1NT, South bids 2♦ (transfer to hearts), North obediently bids 2♥ and South bids 3NT.

ANSWERS:

1. South is the captain, because North's hand is limited by his 1NT opening.
2. North is the captain; he will pass with a minimum, bid game, or occasionally, look for slam with a super hand.
3. South is the captain, because North's hand is limited by the original pass. South can pass or make another appropriate call.

4. South is the captain. After North describes his hand, South will decide where to play.

5. South is the captain, because North has limited his hand.

6. North is the captain, because South's bid has limited his hand.

7. South is the captain. South knows the two hands should be in game, so he bids 3NT. North can pass or bid 4♥ if he prefers that contract.

FORTY-THREE

Learn the Principle of Fast Arrival

"Ye can lead a man to the university, but ye cannot make him think."

—Finley Peter Dunne

FAST ARRIVAL is the concept that the quicker a contract is reached, the weaker the hand that placed the contract. Conversely, the slower the bidding sequence, the stronger the possibility that a higher contract may be the correct level.

This is a helpful idea that has become more popular in recent years, as players have become more sophisticated and scientific in their approach to finding the best contract. It makes sense that the more room you leave to explore during the bidding, the more accurate you can be. There are clearly times when jumping to game or slam is called for, but in these situations it's difficult or impossible to make sure you have reached the proper place.

I have found that this principle is especially valuable when playing a Big Club system (Precision) or Two Over One Game Force (I play Precision along with 2/1). Many of the bids are limited and there are often auctions when you are already forced to game, so you have plenty of bidding space to examine whether you have the resources to be in slam.

Even if you use this principle, there are still many instances when a jump shows a stronger hand than not jumping. So be aware that most of the fast arrival auctions are those when you are already committed to game. In most other auctions, a jump is trying to tell partner that you have extra values, whether after opening the bidding and jumping after partner's response or after a takeout double.

It can be a complicated topic, so it's important to have a solid partnership to use the principle and also to spend plenty of time discussing the various sequences and whether the principle applies.

Here are two examples of fast arrival:

in Precision:

When the bidding starts:

OPENER	RESPONDER
1♣ (At least 16 HCP)	1♠ (8+ HCP, forcing to game)

4♠ is the weakest bid opener can make.

2♠ is the strongest bid opener can make, a trump-asking bid, taking control of the bidding (captain of the ship)

3♠ is somewhere in the middle of the other two bids.

COMPARE THESE TWO AUCTIONS:

WEST	NORTH	EAST	SOUTH
1♠	Pass	2♦	Pass
2♠	Pass	4♠	All Pass

WEST	NORTH	EAST	SOUTH
1♠	Pass	2♦	Pass
2♠	Pass	3♠	All Pass

The second auction shows some slam interest, while the first one doesn't.

FORTY-FOUR

With 3-3 In the Minors, Open 1♣

"Our life is frittered away by detail. Simplify, simplify, simplify."

—Henry David Thoreau

LTHOUGH THERE IS some disagreement among teachers, books and experts about whether to open the bidding 1 ♣ or 1 ♦ when you have four of each, there is a strong consensus that with three in both minors it is better to open 1♣.

This is not the most important decision you will make in your partnership, but it does make sense.

1. It gives you slightly more room to explore and describe your hand during the auction.
2. It is then more likely when you open 1♦ that you have four cards in the suit; this can be helpful later in the auction. So my recommendation is to open 1♦ when you are 4-4 in the minors.
3. Unless you rebid your club suit, your partner won't take your opening bid too seriously. In modern

bridge, a 1♣ opening is considered a catch-all bid to start the bidding when you are playing Standard American or 2 over 1 Game Force, like 1♦ is the catch-all bid when playing the Precision Club or any strong 1♣ system.

4. If you hold say, ♦A-K-J ♣J-9-4 you can always open 1♦ if you choose. This principle is meant as a helpful guideline.

FORTY-FIVE

When You Open the Bidding 1♦ and Rebid the Suit, You Should Have Six Cards in That Suit

BY STEVE WEINSTEIN

"The purpose of education is to replace an empty mind with an open one."

—Malcolm Forbes

ALTHOUGH YOU'RE NOT always dealt the exact hand you would like to have to make bidding easy, you should still try to describe your hand as well as possible for partner. So when you open 1♦ and then bid the suit again on the next round, your partner should expect you to have at least six of them. The difference between having five or six cards in a suit can be significant, especially if your side intends to play in that suit or you are considering 3NT as the final contract.

With five diamonds, if the bidding proceeds:

1♦, 1 of-a-major by partner, on the second round of bidding with about 12–14 HCP you can frequently rebid 1NT (it's a good idea to have at least two cards in your partner's major when you do this). When you have a singleton in partner's suit, it's usually best to find a bid other than 1NT; in these cases, you have the choice of an imperfect bid such as rebidding your suit with five or supporting partner's major with three cards. When you haven't been dealt the perfect hand for your bid, you have to decide to make the "least bad bid," which requires good judgment, a solid education from your teacher and reading helpful books, plus experience.

This is the way I play with Bobby Levin:

Opener can rebid 1NT with a singleton spade, but never a singleton heart. We try to avoid this. Rebidding 2♣ can be a good five-card suit after a 1♣ opener. We are more likely to rebid 1NT with a singleton honor.

When your partner responds one of a major to your one-of-a-minor opener, when should you raise on three-card support? The answer depends on the shape of your hand and where your values are located. I have a detailed article on the Bridge Winners website: 1 minor — 1 Major — Now what? from November, 2010.

STEVE WEINSTEIN is a professional bridge and poker player. He lives in Andes, NY with his wife, Liz, dog Luther and Archie the cat. Steve has 19 NABC victories and is the 2010 World Open Pairs Champion. He holds the record for the youngest-ever winner of an NABC event and also has won the Cavendish more than anyone else. Steve writes for Bridge Winners and has many popular articles on the site. His most recent victory is the Norman Kay Platinum Pairs in Philadelphia.

♤ ♡ ◇ ♧

FORTY-SIX

Reverses Are Sometimes Misunderstood So Learn About Them

BY BARBARA SEAGRAM

"Everything is both simpler than we can imagine and more complicated than we can conceive."

–Goethe

WHAT IS A REVERSE? A reverse occurs when opener rebids a suit at the two level that is higher-ranking than his first bid suit. Here are two standard reverses:

1♣ – 1♠
2♥

or

1♥ – 2♦
2♠

REVERSE RULES:

1. When responder has to make his second bid on the three level to give a preference to opener's first suit, opener has "reversed" the bidding.
2. A reverse always shows an unbalanced hand, at least 5-4 in the two bid suits. The first suit should always be longer than the second-bid suit.
3. It shows at least 16 HCP.
4. Reverses are forcing for one round.
5. When opener has a two-suiter and is not strong enough to reverse, on the second round of bidding he should choose one of these alternatives: bid new suit at the one level, rebid his opening suit, bid a lower-ranking suit at the two level or raise partner's suit.
6. When using the Two over One Game Force system a sequence such as 1♥–2♦–2♠ is still a reverse. Although some play that this sequence doesn't show extra values, I personally believe that it should.

What do you rebid when partner makes a reverse? Remember that a reverse is forcing for one round.

When you have a very weak hand:

1. Bid the minimum number of notrump.
2. Support opener's suit at the lowest level.
3. Rebid your suit at the lowest level.
   All other bids are forcing to game.

NOTE: Be sure to never raise opener's second suit unless you have four-card support.

BARBARA SEAGRAM hails from Barbados, West Indies. She now owns and runs a School of Bridge in Toronto, teaching tens of thousands of students annually. Barbara and her husband Alex travel all over the world teaching bridge and have visited over 150 countries. Their real passions are projects in Africa, Cambodia and Laos, building schools, providing water and teaching English. Barbara has written 24 books, including "25 Bridge Conventions You Should Know," the American Bridge Teachers' Book of the Year. She is also very active in the ABTA and writes a monthly newsletter that she sends out to 5000 of her students.

FORTY-SEVEN

Use Specific Opening Preemptive Bids

Harold: "Maude, do you pray?"
Maude: "No, I communicate."

–From Harold and Maude (1971), my favorite movie

(In the Appendix, I've listed 100 movies that are among my favorites...I'm not a movie expert; I just enjoy going to shows that are well made and play with my emotions. Because this book is about having fun and enjoying life, I've included personal non-bridge-related recommendations that you can explore if you wish).

WHEN YOU OPEN the bidding on the two or three level, make sure you and your partner have discussed the quality of your suit and the limits to your outside cards. For example, I play that I don't open on the three level with an outside ace (in first or second seat). This makes it much easier for my partner to evaluate his hand and decide whether to bid or defend. Occasionally, the opponents will know more about your hand than you would like, but it's a small price to pay for accuracy and partnership cooperation.

Your goal is to put pressure on the opponents to make it difficult for them to reach their optimum contract. It's important to use good judgment, patience and discipline when opening the bidding at the three level, so your partner will have a reasonable chance to make the best decision for your partnership: pass, raise your suit, bid a game or slam, double the opponents or sacrifice. There are many helpful sources to explain the best methods for preemptive bids on the three level.

1. Do you always have a seven-card suit for your bid? Or is it OK to have six or eight cards in your suit?
2. How many honors are required in your suit to open on the three level?
3. What rules will your partnership follow depending on the vulnerability?
4. What agreements do you have about playing strength, distribution, values in other suits, bidding a new suit, and competitive auctions?

These are all issues that you should discuss in a regular partnership. If you are sitting down with a partner for the first time or you have seldom played together, try to quickly agree on sensible, simple methods.

Here are a few personal recommendations:

- The usual rules apply in first or second seat (when partner is an unpassed hand). In third seat, once partner has passed, your rules should be different. It's important to be very aggressive because your LHO in fourth seat possesses the best hand at the table and your job is to make life as difficult as possible for him, while making sure you don't do anything crazy to put your side at unnecessary risk.

- As I explained above, I like to have no outside aces. I used to not have any outside kings, but in recent years I've become more flexible. This allows you to preempt more often while limiting the information available to the opponents that can help them in the play or on defense.

- It's also a good idea to not have a four-card major or a void on the side.

- When it's a close decision whether to open one or three, I tend to open at the one level, because I have confidence in my partnership's good judgment on how high to bid. An additional recommendation: the better the opponents, the more likely I am to preempt to try to disrupt their competitive bidding; weaker pairs might have a hard time reaching the best contract anyway, no matter how high you open the bidding.

- The standard guidelines for preempts are the Rules of Two, Three and Four (at unfavorable vulnerability have approximately seven playing tricks, equal vulnerability six tricks, and favorable vulnerability five tricks). If you are comfortable with these rules, that is fine. Whatever suits your personality and partner is playable; just make sure you discuss whether to be even more solid than these rules, if the guidelines work well for you, or if you choose to be even more aggressive by opening six-card suits or with less playing strength. Some people aren't comfortable sticking their necks out, because they might be chopped off (or doubled); some love to make the opponents uncomfortable and are willing to take extreme risks.

Here are a few quizzes on three-level openings. What would you bid as dealer (would the vulnerability change your bid?).

1. ♠ K Q J 10 9 7 2
   ♥ 7 2
   ♦ 6 4 3
   ♣ 8

2. ♠ Q J 9 8 7 5 2
   ♥ 10 7
   ♦ Q 6 5
   ♣ 5

3. ♠ 4 3
   ♥ K J 10 8 7 4 2
   ♦ Q 5
   ♣ K 7

4. ♠ K Q 8 7 5 4 3
   ♥ A 8 4 2
   ♦ 6
   ♣ 8

5. ♠ Q J 10 6 4 3
   ♥ 8 2
   ♦ A J 9 2
   ♣ 5

6. ♠ 8 7 5
   ♥ –
   ♦ A K J 10 9 4 3
   ♣ Q 6 5

7. ♠ K 9
   ♥ K 5
   ♦ Q 9
   ♣ Q J 9 7 6 3 2

8. ♠ 10 5 3
   ♥ 8
   ♦ K Q J 9 6 5
   ♣ Q J 10

9. ♠ 5
    ♥ K 8
    ♦ A Q J 7 5 4 3
    ♣ 10 9 7

10. ♠ 7
    ♥ K 9 8 7 6 4 2
    ♦ J 10
    ♣ A 10 9

ANSWERS:

1. This is a classic 3♠ opening when you are not vulnerable. When you are vul. vs. NV, and with only six playing tricks, opening 3♠ or passing would depend on your personality and what is comfortable for you and your partnership. Some players might open 2♠, but I like to have specifically six for a weak-two bid (although with certain partners who approve, I might only have five to open two).

2. Not vulnerable, this looks like a good 3♠ bid to me, although in a perfect world you'd like a little better suit. It is, however, too aggressive for most sane partners if you're vulnerable.

3. A good 3♥ opener vulnerable. Extra defense might make some of us a little reluctant to open 3♥, but it is the choice of most experienced players without enough power to open 1♥.

4. A matter of style and personality. Many would shy away from a 3♠ opening with an outside ace AND a four-card heart suit. I totally agree and would never consider opening this 3♠. I use the Rule of 20 (discussed elsewhere in this book), so I have an easy 1♠ opening and nothing to be ashamed of, with 9 high-card points + 11 cards in my two longest suits. I

even have two quick tricks for purists who insist on them to open.

5. Looks like a weak 2♠ bid to me at any vulnerability. Even though I have four diamonds, that wouldn't keep me from opening. This hand breaks my rule for opening 3♠, because of the outside ace.

6. Some would open 3♦, but it's much too good for my taste. With 10 HCP and 10 cards in my two longest suits, it's an easy 1♦ opening at any vulnerability for me. I can continue to rebid my diamonds when I have the chance, so my partner should have an excellent idea of my hand.

7. I hope you counted the high card points and realize that with 11, you really have too much to preempt. Our Rule of 20 allows us to happily open the bidding. Purists who insist on two Quick Tricks will pass unless they add a few points for the length in clubs.

8. This is a reasonable six-card 3♦ opening not vulnerable; vulnerable, most would pass and await developments.

9. A minimum 1♦ opening with 10 HCP and 10 cards in our two longest suits.

10. Although I like to open at the three level as much as anyone, the poor quality of the heart suit along with the outside ace tell me to pass as dealer.

♠ ♡ ◇ ♣

FORTY-EIGHT

Ogust Rebids Are Useful Over Weak Two Bids

"If your mind isn't clouded by unnecessary things, this is the best season of your life."

—Wu-men

WEAK TWO-BIDS are now an essential part of most systems. The number of HCP and the quality of an opening two-bidder's suit are determined by each partnership's preference. So are the responses to a weak two-bid.

- The standard range for most two-bids is about 4–10, 5–10, 6–10 or 5–11 HCP, so it's usually simple to find a comfort zone for your partnership.
- Most players prefer to have six cards in their weak two-bid suit, so it's assumed that is what partner will have. In third seat, as with many bids, five-card suits are more frequent with aggressive and experienced players, but six cards is the norm. (In the old days, I popularized and helped write a system book, "Every Hand an Adventure"—EHAA. We opened almost

any five-card suit with a weak two; it was a lot of fun to play, but we didn't always reach the best contract. Most players are saner these days).

- It's a good idea not to have a side four-card major when you open a weak two. You could have a fit in that major, so don't open a weak two when you are 6-4 or 4-6.

- When partner raises your weak two to the three level, it is competitive and not invitational.

- Most partnerships play that a raise of the weak-two bid is the only non-force (RONF), so new suits are forcing. The opening two-bidder then makes the most descriptive bid(s) to show responder his hand. Once you open a weak two, the responder is the captain. He will make the final decision on how high to bid and what the contract should be.

- If responder doesn't have a raise of the weak-two bidder's suit or a long suit of his own, the best asking bid is 2NT. Many pairs use this bid to ask the opener to describe his hand further. The simplest method is to bid a feature (usually an ace or a king) or rebid the opening suit with a weak hand.

- There are various other methods to inquire about opener's hand. My favorite is called Ogust, devised by Harold Ogust of New York, founder of Goren International. I think these bids give you the most useful information over weak twos. When responder bids 2NT, the opener answers:

    3♣ weak hand (low end of the HCP range), weak suit

    3♦ weak hand, strong suit

3♥ strong hand, weak suit

3♠ strong hand(top of the range), strong suit

3NT a solid suit (A-K-Q-x-x-x or better)

- What you consider a "weak" or "strong" holding depends on your partnership's rules for HCP and the weak-two bidder's suit quality. Some pairs like a semi-solid holding such as A-Q-10-8-7-4 and others will open with K-10-7-5-4-2. It depends on what you and partner prefer.

Here are a few quizzes on Ogust rebids:

You open 2♠ and Partner bids 2NT (Ogust). What do you respond with these hands?

1.	♠ K Q J 8 6 4	2.	♠ A K Q 10 6 5
	♥ 8 5		♥ 8 5 2
	♦ 9 7		♦ 3
	♣ 6 4 3		♣ 10 8 5
3.	♠ A 9 6 5 3 2	4.	♠ Q 9 8 6 5 2
	♥ 6 4		♥ Q J 6
	♦ K Q 3		♦ 10 8 7
	♣ 9 8		♣ 4

ANSWERS:

1. 3♦ weak hand, strong suit
2. 3NT solid suit
3. 3♥ strong hand, weak suit
4. 3♣ weak hand, weak suit

There are also Modified Ogust rebids if you open five-card weak-two bids and/or sometimes have four-card side suits. A helpful explanation is available in Kearse's (out of print) "Bridge Conventions Complete."

FORTY-NINE

Sometimes It's a Good Idea to Bid the Suit in Which You Are Weak

"Oh, what a tangled web we weave when first we practice to deceive!"

—Sir Walter Scott

ALTHOUGH it's usually excellent advice to show your partner the distribution and strength of your hand by bidding accurately, there are occasions when it is helpful to ignore this principle.

A situation I like to exploit is when it appears the final contract will be 3NT and our side has extra values: enough to make 3NT but probably not enough for slam. Our combined assets are about 28 to 31 high card points. It is easier to use the auction to your advantage when partner has opened the bidding with a limited hand (such as 1NT with 12–14 or 15–17 points) or you are playing the Precision Club so the opening bid is limited to 15 (unless you open 1♣).

The classic auction is when partner opens 1♦ and your weakest suit is clubs. Then 1♦ / 2♣ / partner's rebid and finally 3NT by you will almost always bring a major-suit opening lead. It's especially effective is you have strong holdings in the majors; sometimes you will receive a lead that puts you a trick ahead of the field.

Another auction that can be used similarly is 1NT / 3NT when you have a four- or five-card major. At matchpoints, when your side has close to 30 HCP, you might make an extra trick at notrump or make 5NT when you can only make five of the major (In a team game, the extra points are unimportant, so this strategy should be avoided). However, once you realize that strategy at matchpoints is different from other forms of bridge, you just might want to keep this bid in your arsenal and occasionally spring it on the unsuspecting opponents.

FIFTY

If You Know Where to Play the Contract, Just Go Ahead and Bid It

"The more complex the mind, the greater the need for simplicity."

–Mr. Spock on *Star Trek*

THIS RULE seems so simple, but it is violated frequently at the table. Bidding is (usually) not an exact science, so when you are fairly sure that you know where to play the hand, go ahead and place the final contract. You won't always be correct, but it is much better than making a bid that you partner may misunderstand, having an awkward or unsuccessful auction, having your partner pass when you meant a bid as forcing, or giving the opponents more information.

That is one of the reasons I enjoy playing the Precision Club so much. When my partner opens a limited (11–15 high card points) 1♦, 1♥, 1♠ or 2♣, it is frequently easy to simply bid 3NT without giving away any further information. This obviously makes the opponent's opening lead more difficult, and his choice can be the difference between a successful contract and being defeated. It also feels good to not have to worry about a complicated sequence; we can save our brains for future hands.

I have heard this called the Hamman Rule, along with other wise principles that he has given the bridge world over the years. In Mike Lawrence's "Judgment 2", there is a Hamman Rule about a winning attitude: "After a good result, stop reveling in it. After a terrible result, stop fretting about it." He has another "rule" that is similar to my principle: If you're wondering what to bid and 3NT is one of the options, bid it. As one of the world's best and most innovative players, Bob could probably have his own Ten Bridge Commandments, so I'll attribute it to him. Whenever this rule doesn't work out, it's easy for me to think he would have made the same bid, so that's a good enough reason for me.

♠ ♡ ◇ ♣

FIFTY-ONE

When You have a Misfit, Stop Bidding as Soon as Possible

"A white flower grows in the quietness. Let your tongue become that flower."

–Rumi

ALTHOUGH WE WANT to reach game or slam when our side has most of the high-card points in the deck, sometimes the two hands don't fit together well and the resulting auction can be very difficult and frustrating. When there is a fit of at least eight cards available between the two hands, we can usually find an acceptable place to play. Even when the final contract is 3NT, the play goes more smoothly when transportation between the two hands is reasonable. However, when a misfit is apparent during the bidding, good judgment is needed to stop at a low level when the two hands don't fit well. When you are say, 5-5 or 5-4 in two suits and as your partner, I'm dealt the other two suits as my longest ones, the bidding sequence can become a battle between us.

When you have shortness in partner's suit or suits, it's time to be careful and consider that this deal could be a misfit. Caution is called for. It's even more apparent that it's a dangerous situation when you are in a competitive auction and you have shortness is your partner's suit(s) along with length in the opponents' suit.

Aggressive bidding is usually productive, but on misfits, it is easy to become carried away and reach a contract that has no chance. Even very accomplished and experienced players can go astray in the bidding. There is no magic bullet to avoid a disaster when you have a misfit. The only solution is to stop bidding as soon as you sense that the two hands don't fit together well.

Here are a few examples to illustrate this advice:

1.
♠ A J 10 6 5
♥ 8
♦ K Q 7 6
♣ J 4 3

The bidding has proceeded:

PARTNER	YOU
1♥	1♠
2♥	?

What is your correct bid?

You have 11 HCP and so many players would venture 2NT. However, at any form of scoring, it's unlikely that you will make game, mostly because of the singleton heart in your hand. The only logical action is to pass. Your partner could have the perfect hand to make 3NT or it could be a lucky deal. The point is that it is clearly against the odds to bid 2NT, so try to turn this hand into a plus score for a probable good result. Just pass.

When you and partner have different long suits, beware. Especially against solid defenders, you can have awful transportation problems and have a frustrating result.

2. You hold:

♠ 8
♥ A J 10 6 5
♦ 4 3
♣ A Q 9 4 2

and the bidding proceeds:

PARTNER	YOU
1♠	1NT (forcing)
2♦	2♥
3♦	?

What is your best call?

A pass is very likely your winning call. You may make 3NT, especially if partner has the ♣K or ♣J-10, but most of partner's points are probably in his two suits and game is against the odds.

3. Your hand is:

♠ Q 8 3 2
♥ 5
♦ A Q 8
♣ A Q 9 8 4

The bidding has proceeded:

YOU	LHO	PARTNER	RHO
1♣	Pass	1♥	Pass
1♠	Pass	2♥	Pass

What is your best call now? Many players would try 2NT, because they have a singleton in partner's suit and they assume notrump is a better spot than 2♥. However, you should pass. It's a good idea to avoid playing in notrump when you have little or no support for partner's suit and insufficient HCP. 2♥ could easily be your last chance for a plus score. 2NT should be a hopeful invitation, not an attempt to rescue partner from a low-level contract when you have an apparent misfit.

♤ ♡ ◇ ♧

FIFTY-TWO

Don't Use the Blackwood Convention When You Have a Void

"A moment's insight is sometimes worth a life's experience."

—Oliver Wendell Holmes

I HAVE SEEN this rule violated many times, especially at clubs by novices or inexperienced partnerships. Blackwood is a wonderful tool when all you need to know is how many aces and/or kings your partner has. It is not useful when you might lose the first two tricks in a suit or when you have a void. In these situations, you cannot tell by using Blackwood if your partnership has the crucial ace or aces. Learning to cue bid well is a key to improving your game. There are many excellent books to help you learn this valuable concept, so take advantage of the expert advice that is available to you.

Here is an example of the proper way to investigate slam when you have a void:

Let's say you hold the following hand:

♠ —
♥ A Q J 8 7 5 4
♦ K 5 4
♣ K Q 7

and after you open 1♥, you partner makes a limit raise of 3♥. Partner probably has one or two aces; if you bid Blackwood, the answer won't solve your problem because you need to know which ace or aces your partner has in addition to how many.

If your partner has one ace and it's in diamonds or clubs, you should be cold or at least a huge favorite to make 6♥. But if it's the ♠A you'll very likely lose two tricks and go down in your slam.

If your partner has two aces and they are both in the minors, it looks like you can count on 13 tricks for the grand slam; if one is the ♠A, six is the limit.

Here's another example:

Your hand is:

♠ 8 5
♥ A J 9 5 3 2
♦ A K Q 10 4
♣ —

Partner makes a limit raise in hearts to 3♥. You cue bid 4♣ and partner cue bids 4♠. Now you can be confident that you will make at least a small slam; if you had bid Blackwood, your partner might have most of his values in clubs and slam wouldn't be so likely. This hand is much easier to bid if you are cuebidding only first-round control instead of the alternative of showing first or second round control. Sometimes one method is better for a particular hand (showing first-round control only or showing first- or second-round control). Make sure to discuss your preference with your partner, so you are using the same cuebids.

So what's the solution to your dilemma? Instead of automatically using Blackwood, learn to cue bid your controls (aces, kings, singletons and voids) so your partnership will know which aces you have and which ones the opponents have. Cue bidding is a very complex topic and not all slam decisions once you cue bid will be as easy as the above example. However, it is a tool that top players use to their advantage, while many less-experienced players have little understanding of cue bidding and have seldom or never made one.

If you always use Blackwood (even with a void) or jump to slam because you aren't sure how to proceed when you have a void, this is a perfect time to add cue bidding to your system.

Note: There is an advanced method to investigate slam when one partner has made a splinter bid and then uses the Blackwood Convention. This is called Exclusion Blackwood and should only be used when the shortness is a void. The partner of the splinter bidder excludes from his Blackwood answer the suit in which the shortness has been shown.

FIFTY-THREE

Roman Keycard Blackwood Is Worthwhile for Experienced Partnerships

A little learning is a dangerous thing."

–Alexander Pope

L EARN ROMAN Keycard Blackwood to improve your slam bidding and to stay out of ones you should avoid. Key Card Blackwood was the first to count the king of trumps as the fifth ace. In recent years, most experienced players have adopted the Roman version. It is just as easy to learn and it is more accurate. Whatever version you play instead of standard old-fashioned Blackwood, make sure you discuss all the details with your partner.

Although there are various methods to identify the trump suit, here is a simple rule that works well with Roman Key Card Blackwood. If you have agreed upon a suit, obviously that is the trump suit and the fifth ace is the king of that suit. If you haven't agreed upon a trump suit in the auction, the trump suit (for the purpose of finding out about the fifth ace, the trump king) is the last suit bid before the

4NT asking bid. This is the way I play RKCB. Some players have other rules, such as designating the trump suit as responder's suit if he jump shifts and then bids notrump on his next turn. This is a discussion you and your partner should have before including RKCB in your system.

The two most popular options are now 3014 or 1430 (They are usually called "Thirty-fourteen" and "Fourteen-thirty"). One doesn't have a huge advantage over the other.

With 3014, the responses to 4NT are:

5♣   0 or 3 Keycards
5♦   1 or 4 Keycards
5♥   2 Keycards without the Trump Queen
5♠   2 Keycards with the Trump Queen

When you use 1430, the 5♣ and 5♦ responses are reversed.

You can then find out about the Trump Queen after a 5♣ or 5♦ response to 4NT. The next step inquires about the queen and there are two currently popular responses to this:

Method A:

1. The first step denies the queen of trump.
2. The second step shows the queen of trump.

Method B (which is more complicated, but also gives more information). The next step still asks about the Trump Queen, but there are more responses:

1. 5 of the agreed upon trump suit denies the queen
2. 6 of the trump suit shows the queen of trumps, but denies having any kings.
3. Any other bid shows the trump queen and shows the cheapest king.

Depending on which methods you use, you also should have a specific agreement on responses when the 4NT bidder next calls 5NT. Many experts show specific kings, starting with the lowest ranking, while others simply show the number of kings (excluding the king of trump).

There is also a reasonable version of RKCB called Kickback that saves space in the auction. Jeff Rubens of *Bridge World* magazine first wrote about it in 1981. The bid immediately above four of the agreed suit is the asking bid: If clubs are the trump suit, 4♦ is the asking bid; if diamonds are agreed, 4♥ is the asking bid; if hearts are agreed, 4♠ is the asking bid. Then five of the Kickback suit is searching for a grand slam, showing all five keycards and the queen of trump, asking for specific kings.

Here are a few quizzes for RKCB. After partner opens 1♥, you respond 3♥, and then he bids 4NT, what would you respond to his bid (let's assume you are playing 3014):

1.   ♠ A J 6 4   2.   ♠ J
      ♥ K J 9 3   ♥ K Q 10 8
      ♦ 10 5   ♦ Q J 7 5
      ♣ 6 5 3   ♣ J 10 9 7

3.   ♠ A Q 4 2   4.   ♠ K Q 7 6
      ♥ K Q 7 6   ♥ Q J 9 8
      ♦ 8 7 3   ♦ K 10 3
      ♣ J 3   ♣ 8 6

ANSWERS:

1. 5♥   2 Key Cards without the queen
2. 5♦   1 or 4 Key Cards
3. 5♠   2 Key Cards with the queen
4. 5♣   0 or 3 Key Cards

FIFTY-FOUR

Learn Cuebidding to Make Sure You Don't Have Two Quick Losers in a Suit When You Are Looking for Slam

"Experience is a hard teacher, because she gives the test first, the lesson afterward."

—Vernon Law

BESIDES BEING HELPFUL when one partner has a void, a cue bid is a brilliant way to find out when your side has two quick losers in a suit. This is another occasion when you should absolutely not use Blackwood, so you have a scientific way to determine if slam is likely to make. When you have enough assets, there are many deals when slam is a good bet when the opponents can't take two quick tricks in a suit. By cue bidding, you can obtain the necessary information to ensure you are likely to make a slam.

Here is an example hand:

Let's say you hold:

♠ A K 7
♥ A K 10 9 7 5
♦ 9 5
♣ A 4

Partner makes a limit raise in hearts to 3♥. You could be cold for 6 or 7 hearts, but you could also be off the first two diamond tricks. The solution is to cue bid 4♣ and hopefully partner will be able to cue bid 4♦. If partner can't bid 4♦, you should settle for game at 4♥. If partner does cue bid 4♦, you can now use Blackwood to see how many aces he has. This is a logical, simple auction that is important to use when necessary.

Following are a few valuable rules to help you navigate through the subject of cue bidding:

- Find several authoritative articles and books on the subject. Every partnership has their own guidelines on when to cue bid and exactly which methods they prefer. One of the key choices you should make is whether you cue bid only first-round controls (aces and voids) or include second-round controls (kings and singletons). There are valid schools of thought for both approaches, so educating yourself will enable you to decide on your preference.
- Make sure to sit down with your partner(s) so you agree on how to handle cue bidding. It is a complicated subject. If you can master the basics so

that you can feel somewhat comfortable showing controls, you deserve a pat on the back.

- Once you have established a fit at the level of three of-a-major or above, a new suit is a control-showing cue bid.
- You can use your preferred form of Blackwood after a cue bidding sequence to confirm the number of aces your partner holds and/or to investigate further for the best contract.

FIFTY-FIVE

Discuss with Your Partner When 4♣ Clubs Is Gerber

"It's what you learn after you know it all that counts."

–John Wooden

ALTHOUGH BLACKWOOD is the most frequently used convention when exploring for slams, Gerber can also be helpful. It is relied on much more by less-experienced players than by experts who tend to use 4♣ for other purposes such as cue bids and splinter bids. At bridge clubs, there are many players who bring out Gerber in most slam auctions. No matter if you're a huge fan of the bid or use it sparingly, it's important to know when 4♣ is Gerber and when it's something else.

The most important advantage of Gerber is that you can determine how many aces you have without bidding past game, while Blackwood will take you to the five level.

The responses to Gerber are similar to Blackwood:

4♦	=	0 or 4 aces
4♥	=	1 ace
4♠	=	2 aces
4NT	=	3 aces

I use Gerber in my partnership in very specific auctions, after no trump is bid and there is a jump to 4♣:

OPENER	RESPONDER
1NT	4♣
2NT	4♣
1♣ or 1♦	2NT
4♣	
1♣ or 1♦	1♥ or 1♠
2NT	4♣

In other auctions, 4♣ has another meaning for us. However, if you prefer, there are various other auctions you can designate as Gerber such as those below. You can even decide that any time that you agree on a trump suit, 4♣ is Gerber (although I prefer to use this as a cue bid):

OPENER	RESPONDER
1NT	2♣ (Stayman)
2♥ or 2♠	4♣
1♥ or 1♠	2♣ or 2♦
3NT	4♣
1♥ or 1♠	3♥ or 3♠
4♣	

As with Blackwood, if you bid 5♣ over the ace-showing response to 4♣, your side should possess all four aces.

There are also more complicated methods such as Roman Gerber, Key Card Gerber, Black and Red Gerber and Super Gerber.

FIFTY-SIX

Splinter Bids Are Useful if You Have a Solid Partnership

BY DOROTHY HAYDEN TRUSCOTT

"When the student is ready, the teacher will appear."

–Buddha

IN THE EARLY SIXTIES I DEVELOPED a convention which was described in the first edition of *BID BETTER, PLAY BETTER* under the heading of "THE UNUSUAL JUMP TO SHOW A SINGLETON." It proved so popular that it is now used by the vast majority of experienced players. Today it is known as the SPLINTER BID.

Why is a Splinter used? It is a tool to explore for slam. By guaranteeing a fit and allowing the partnership to evaluate a crucial side suit, a pair can sometimes bid to a good slam with fewer than the usual number of HCP and an excellent trump fit. Splinters also help to avoid poor slams when there is duplication of values.

What is required to make a Splinter? It promises:

1. At least four-card support for partner's last bid suit.
2. A singleton or void in the Splinter suit.
3. A hand that is at least good enough for game.

WEST	EAST
♠ A K 8 7 5 2	♠ J 9 6 4
♥ 8	♥ A Q 7 6
♦ K Q 7	♦ A J 8 6
♣ 8 7 4	♣ 9

1♠	4♣
4NT	5♥
6♠	Pass

East's jump to four clubs is a splinter bid. It shows a forcing raise in spades which includes a singleton (or void) in clubs. West has no wasted values in clubs and is able to picture a slam if partner has two aces. Notice that East-West have a combined total of only 24 HCP. Without the splinter bid it would be very difficult for them to even consider slam.

The chief value of the splinter bid is, of course, to get you to slam when partner has a singleton opposite your worthless holding. An additional, and very substantial benefit, however, is to keep you out of slam when partner has a singleton opposite your strength.

WEST	EAST
♠ A Q 9 8 7	♠ K J 10 5 2
♥ A	♥ K J 7
♦ K Q 7	♦ 2
♣ J 8 6 2	♣ A 5 4 3

1♠	4♦
4♠	Pass

This time East has shown at least four-card spade support, a hand worth 13-16, and a singleton (or void) in diamonds. West mentally tears up his king and queen of diamonds and is just able to put on the brakes.

WARNING: When responder has a singleton heart the bidding is:

WEST	EAST
1♠	4♥

This is deceptive. West might think partner had eight hearts and wished to play there. It is a good idea to discuss this exact auction with partner before you use it. Point out to him that if you really wanted to play four hearts you could bid two hearts first and then four hearts next round.

Suppose the opening bid is one heart. Four clubs and four diamonds show the singleton in a minor. With a singleton spade you bid three spades. Again, this should be discussed with partner before you use it. He might think you had something like:

♠ K Q 9 8 6 5 2
♥ 8
♦ 8 7 4
♣ 9 5

Point out to him that if you did have the weak hand with seven spades you would bid one spade first, then sign off in two spades and if there were another round of bidding you would sign off again in three spades.

Splinters work well in this situation:

WEST	EAST
♠ A J 10 6	♠ K Q 8 5 4
♥ A Q	♥ 9 2
♦ K Q J 9 8 7	♦ A 5 2
♣ 8	♣ J 7 5
1♦	1♠
4♣	4♦
4♥	4NT
5♥	6♠

West opens the bidding with 1♦ and is delighted to hear partner respond 1♠. He decides there is a game even if East has a measly six points. If he were not playing splinters he would have to bid four spades at this point, saying, "I have four trumps for you, partner, and a hand worth about 20." Playing splinters, however, he bids 4♣ which is much more descriptive. It says, "I have four trumps for you, partner, and a hand worth about 20 with a singleton or void in clubs." East now bids 4♦ showing the diamond ace and slam interest. West cue bids the heart ace and East is off to the races.

Bonus Mileage

Those who play splinters can get more mileage by agreeing that in sequences such as:

WEST	EAST
1♣	1♠
4♠	

West is denying a singleton.

DOROTHY TRUSCOTT, who died in 2006, was one of the world's leading players. She won the Venice Cup three times, the World Olympiad Women's Teams and more than 30 national titles. Dorothy was the author of two classic books: "Bid Better, Play Better" and "Winning Declarer Play."

FIFTY-SEVEN

Don't Bid a Grand Slam Unless You Can Count All 13 Tricks

"He who is greedy is always in want."

—Horace

THIS IS VERY SOUND ADVICE whether you are playing in a duplicate game, Swiss teams or knockout. The history of bridge is filled with many examples of someone bidding a grand slam that didn't make. Surprisingly, even if you can take all the tricks, on more occasions than you would expect, simply bidding the small slam would earn your partnership a positive result or at worst a push board. Even though you might think that the small slam is easy to bid, anything could happen at the other table in a team game or throughout the field at matchpoints. There might be a bidding misunderstanding or possibly aggressive preemptive and/or competitive bidding. Other pairs may not have the tools to bid as well as you and your competent partner. This is a rule that holds true even at the highest levels of the game.

It's not difficult to find example hands demonstrating this principle in world championships, so I will share four with you.

1. In the 2004 Olympiad in Istanbul, Turkey the Italian pair of Lauria and Versace reached 7♦ on this hand with the following complicated auction.

Board 52 • Dealer: West • All Vulnerable

♠ A
♥ A 5 3
♦ A Q 10 9 5 2
♣ A K 7

♠ Q 9 3 2
♥ Q 9 8 6
♦ J 7
♣ 9 6 3

♠ 10 8 7 6
♥ 10 4
♦ 8 4 3
♣ Q 5 4 2

♠ K J 5 4
♥ K J 7 2
♦ K 6
♣ J 10 8

WEST	NORTH	EAST	SOUTH
Pass	1♦	Pass	1♥
Pass	2♠ (i)	Pass	2NT (ii)
Pass	3♣ (iii)	Pass	3♦ (iv)
Pass	4♣ (v)	Pass	4♦ (vi)
Pass	4♥ (vi)	Pass	4♠ (vi)
Pass	4NT	Pass	5♦ (vii)
Pass	5♠ (viii)	Pass	5NT
Pass	7♦	All Pass	

Explanation of bids on previous page:

(i) 16+ with 6+ diamonds or both red suits; (ii) Relay; (iii) Three hearts; (iv) Fit; (v) Slam try; (vi) Cuebid; (vii) One key card; (viii) Grand Slam invitation

The American men (Rosenberg and Zia) had a Standard American auction to the same contract. Although the contract had reasonable chances, the contract failed at both tables. In another match, Pakistan vs. England, the English gained 12 IMPs by bidding 6NT while the Pakistani pair languished in 3NT.

2. Also in the 2004 Olympiad, the Polish women played the USA. The hand is shown below:

Board 80 • Dealer: West • E/W Vulnerable

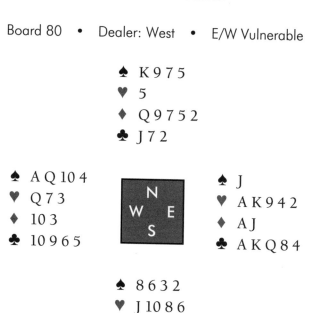

♠ K 9 7 5
♥ 5
♦ Q 9 7 5 2
♣ J 7 2

♠ A Q 10 4   ♠ J
♥ Q 7 3   ♥ A K 9 4 2
♦ 10 3   ♦ A J
♣ 10 9 6 5   ♣ A K Q 8 4

♠ 8 6 3 2
♥ J 10 8 6
♦ K 8 6 4
♣ 3

USA - POLAND

WEST	NORTH	EAST	NORTH
Meyers	Brewiak	Montin	Sarniak
Pass	Pass	2♣	Pass
2♦	Pass	2♥ (i)	Pass
2♠	Pass	3♣ (ii)	Pass
4♠ (iii)	Pass	4NT	Pass
5♠ (iii)	Pass	6♣	Pass
7♣	All Pass		

(i) Kokish
(ii) Hearts and clubs (5-5)
(iii) RKCB

Although 7♣ is an excellent contract, the American women reached it and unluckily went down one. At the other table, the Polish pair reached only 4♥, so this was a huge swing (Bidding 6♣ would have made a 30 IMP difference).

WEST	NORTH	EAST	NORTH
Miszewska	Molson	Banaszk'wicz	Sokolow
Pass	Pass	1♣	Pass
1♠	Pass	2♥	Pass
4♥	All pass		

3. In the 2009 World Championships in Sao Paulo, Brazil in the USA vs. Norway match, both tables reached 7♣ on this hand. It was a good grand slam

but not cold; both declarers suffered defeat; Norway was down one and the Americans down two.

Board 24 • Dealer: West • None Vulnerable

```
                    ♠ J 8 6 5 3
                    ♥ K J 8 2
                    ♦ Q
                    ♣ 9 6 5
  ♠ 4                              ♠ A Q 2
  ♥ A Q 10 5          N            ♥ 9 4
  ♦ A K J 5 3      W     E         ♦ 10 9
  ♣ J 8 7             S            ♣ A K Q 10 4 3
                    ♠ K 10 9 7
                    ♥ 7 6 3
                    ♦ 8 7 6 4 2
                    ♣ 2
```

WEST	NORTH	EAST	SOUTH
Austberg	Hamman	Saelensminde	Zia
1♦	Pass	2♣	Pass
2♥	Pass	3♣	Pass
4♣	Pass	4♠	Pass
4NT	Pass	5♣	Pass
5♦	Pass	7♣	All Pass

WEST	NORTH	EAST	SOUTH
Rodwell	Lindqvist	Meckstroth	Brogeland
1♦	Pass	2♣	Pass
2♦	Pass	2♠	Pass
4♣	Pass	4♦	Pass
4NT	Pass	5♥	Pass
7♣	All Pass		

4. In the November, 2014 Bulletin the Women's Knockout Teams final at the Summer NABC in Las Vegas is covered. The hand below was a pivotal deal:

Dealer: East   •   Both Vulnerable

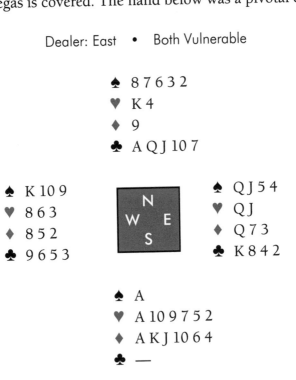

```
              ♠ 8 7 6 3 2
              ♥ K 4
              ♦ 9
              ♣ A Q J 10 7

  ♠ K 10 9           N           ♠ Q J 5 4
  ♥ 8 6 3        W       E       ♥ Q J
  ♦ 8 5 2            S           ♦ Q 7 3
  ♣ 9 6 5 3                      ♣ K 8 4 2

              ♠ A
              ♥ A 10 9 7 5 2
              ♦ A K J 10 6 4
              ♣ —
```

The Americans played in 5♦ and took all 13 tricks for +640. The Chinese reached an unlikely 7♥ contract (they had a bidding misunderstanding) which came home when the doubleton Q-J of hearts fell and the diamond suit also behaved. Although the grand slam was successful, it's another example showing that you never know what will happen at the other table. China won this match by 1 IMP, so the bridge gods were smiling on them despite their inaccurate bidding.

MATCHPOINTS: At your club or even playing in a tournament, you have the luxury of knowing that most of the weaker and less experienced pairs will be unlikely to bid a grand slam, even if there are 13 tricks readily available.

At IMPs, it can be demoralizing to your team or be the difference between winning and losing a match when you go down in a grand slam. The higher the probability that you will win the match (whether it's because you are the superior team or you have gotten off to a good start in the match), the surer you should be that the grand slam will make. These tactical considerations should always be part of your calculations on slam bidding.

Always be aware that the bridge gods can be harsh even when you are in a great grand slam. In the March 2018 *Bridge World* magazine, two of the best pairs in the world bid to 7♠ with the following hands:

♠ A Q 10 9 7 6 4	♠ K 8
♥ 5 4	♥ A K Q 8 6
♦ 10 3	♦ A
♣ 9 7	♣ A K Q 6 4

One pair even had to overcome annoying preempts to reach the grand by an excellent auction. Alas, even though the only layout to defeat 7♠ was for North to have all 4 spades, it happened on this occasion. Realistically, this is a grand slam that almost everyone would want to reach, so I have much sympathy for these pairs.

FIFTY-EIGHT

Give Two Over One Game Force a Try

"As you grow older, you'll find the only things you regret are the things you didn't do."

–Zachery Scott

WHEN I LEARNED BRIDGE at the University of Florida in 1970, it seemed like everyone was playing the Precision Club. The system was winning high-level championships frequently and it was so popular, Precision could have been considered a fad. That's why I've never understood Standard American very well. From the start, I didn't have much experience playing it, so I'm somewhat uncomfortable when my partner insists on playing Standard.

After using limited opening bids for decades, it's still frustrating for me to have to navigate an auction when the opening bid shows anywhere from 11–12 to 19–20 HCP. The other sequence that I've never liked is one of-a-major and then a two of-a-minor response. Sometimes the response shows 10+ points and sometimes enough for game or more. This just doesn't make sense to me.

Personally, it feels so helpful to know that you are forced to game after a 2 over 1 response. There is room to investigate the best contract and we can both show distribution and strength.

My preference is to play a Big Club system (Precision) along with 2 over 1 Game Force. They meld together perfectly and make most auctions easier. But if you don't want to try Precision, why not try 2 over 1?

Two over one bidding sequences refer to these 6 auctions:

1. 1♦ 2♣
2. 1♥ 2♣
3. 1♥ 2♦
4. 1♠ 2♣
5. 1♠ 2♦
6. 1♠ 2♥

Now that I've sung the praises of the 2 over 1 system, it's important to give you the downside: When you don't have enough to make a 2 over 1 bid, you will often respond with 1NT Forcing. It's the worst part of the system, because it can lead to various inaccurate or awkward auctions. There are specific rules to help you reach the best contract after 1NT Forcing, but no system is perfect. You should study these sequences, so your partnership understands all of the options when you don't have enough to force to game. To help you, some of the best authors in the world share their expertise.

There are a number of popular books to help you learn including:

- *Improve Your 2/1 Game Force Bidding* by Marty Bergen
- *Two Over One: An Introduction* by Steve Bruno & Max Hardy
- *Larry Cohen Teaches 2/1*
- *Two Over One Game Force* by Audrey Grant & Eric Rodwell
- *Two Over One Game Force* by Max Hardy
- *Workbook on the 2 Over 1 System* by Mike Lawrence
- Barbara *Seagram's 2/1 Cheat Sheet*
- *25 Steps to Learning 2/1* by Paul Thurston

$$\spadesuit \ \heartsuit \ \diamondsuit \ \clubsuit$$

FIFTY-NINE

Consider The Precision Club

BY BRENT MANLEY

"In football as in watchmaking, talent and elegance mean nothing without rigor and precision."

–Lionel Messi

I HAVE BEEN PLAYING BRIDGE since 1970, and I discovered duplicate in 1975. Somewhere along the line as I developed as a player, I discovered Precision, a dynamic bidding system that is used today by more and more top players. There are as many variations of the system as there are partnerships – and there are lots of them.

Some players have resisted trying Precision because they believe it to be overly complicated. In some of the variations, there are some fancy, somewhat inscrutable relays, but these elements are not necessary for successful use of the basic system.

In the end, Precision is a very natural system. True, the opening bid of 1♣ is artificial, showing a hand of at least 16 high-card points. Some partnerships agree that if the hand is balanced, the minimum HCP should be 17. The 1♦ response to an opening bid of 1♣ is also artificial, showing

0-7 HCP. Some prefer 0-8 so that any positive response promises a minimum of 9 HCP.

Other responses are natural. For example, a 1♥ response to an opening bid of 1♣ shows five or more hearts and 8 or 9 HCP (depending on your agreements). A response of 1NT shows a balanced hand with 8–13 HCP. Opener can check on four-card majors by bidding 2♣. This should be easy for most players.

There are asking bids that the partnership uses to check on the quality of suits, but these are simple and straightforward. For example, if the bidding goes 1♣ - Pass - 1♥ - Pass, a bid of 2♥ in many systems asks about responder's heart suit. Replies are in steps: 1♠ would show at best five or more hearts to the jack; 1NT would show five hearts to one of the top three honors; 2♣ five to two of the top three, and so forth, up to five or more to the A-K-Q. It's comforting to know something like that, don't you think?

When you play Precision, opponents often try to take advantage of the 1♣ opener to make life tough for you, so it is important to have solid agreements about how to handle interference. These methods are also relatively simple and easy to remember. There's no question the 1♣ opener is sometimes vulnerable to aggressive interference. Remember, however, that the penalty double can solve a lot of these problems.

These are some of the aspects of the Precision system to be aware of if you are thinking about giving it a try. There are some important elements to consider that argue in favor of making the switch. To wit:

1. When your partner opens the bidding, you know a lot about his hand whether he opens a strong 1♣ or some other bid. If partner opens with, say, 1♥, you know the upper limit of his hand is 15 HCP. If you have a poor hand, you know that game is out of the question, so you don't waste bidding space — while providing information to the opponents — trying for something that isn't there.

2. On the other hand, when you have a good hand yourself — say 10 or more HCP — you know game, maybe more, is likely on for your side when partner opens 1♣.

   The asking bids can help you decide whether to try for slam after a positive response or sign off quickly in game. For example, you open 1♣ and partner bids 1♠, forcing to game. You raise (asking about his spade suit) and partner's response shows a jack-high suit. If you have something like ♠Q-x-x, you know slam is not making. No need to make any more bids that will help the defense.

   Although the system is very efficient, there are a couple of aspects you will need to get used to. The top example is the opening bid of 1♦, showing 11–15 HCP and a possible doubleton. This is kind of a catchall bid that you use when you don't have the right hand for an opening bid of 1♣, 1♥ or 1♠. Precision is, after all, a five-card major system.

   You may worry about making an opening bid on a doubleton, but I have been tracking my 1♦ openers for many years and have found that I am more likely to have five diamonds than two for my 1♦ openers.

You will also have to get used to opening 2♣ (natural, usually showing at least six cards in the suit) on a hand with 11–15 HCP. The system for coping with this bid is relatively simple.

You may be asking, "What do I do when I have an opening hand and only one diamond? Do I really have to open on a singleton?" The answer is no: You open 2♦, which shows 11–15 HCP and a singleton or void in diamonds. A common hand for this opening is four spades, four hearts, a singleton diamond and four clubs. The hand can also be 4-3 in the majors with five clubs.

Another reason I like Precision is how well it works in getting to slams. Your asking bids eliminate much of the guesswork that non-Precision players experience when they think slam might be on but can't be sure.

That's my sales pitch. I hope you will think about giving Precision a chance. If you know any players who use the system, ask them why they play it and why they like it. Good luck!

BRENT MANLEY spent 20 years in the newspaper business — as a reporter and an editor — before joining the staff of the American Contract Bridge League in 1989. He was chief editor of the *Bridge Bulletin* at the time of his retirement in 2014 after 25 years with the ACBL. He lives in the Memphis TN area. He is the author of eight books on bridge with another in the works.

RANDY: I've read every book ever written on the Precision Club and "Precision Today" by David Berkowitz and Brent is the one I use currently. It's easy to understand, but also has excellent advice for more sophisticated Precision players.

$$\spadesuit \ \heartsuit \ \diamondsuit \ \clubsuit$$

SIXTY

Learn the Differences in Duplicate Between Matchpoints and Swiss Teams/Knockout Events (IMPs)

"Who do you think were the two best heavyweights who ever fought? I don't really care who you pick, but take those two fighters, both at the peak of their careers, put them in a ring and let them slug it out for 15 rounds. Whoever wins is the champ. That's IMPs. Now take the same two fighters, blindfold them and tie one hand behind their backs. Divide the ring diagonally with a solid barrier and put a heavyweight on each side of the barrier. Now go down to the local tavern and collect 20 drunks. Place 10 drunks on each side of the ring and let the fighters go at it. Whoever knocks out his drunks first is the winner. That's matchpoints!"

–Bob Hamman

WHICH IS THE MORE skillful form of bridge, IMPs or matchpoints? As with art, sports and other aspects of life, beauty is in the eye of the beholder. Each form of bridge is challenging in its own way and if you prefer one over the other, it's a combination of your personality, skill, track record, partnerships and system. Generally, you earn what you deserve at IMPs (at least most of the time, although when you lose a match on a 4-0 break in a grand slam, you might disagree). At matchpoints, there is usually more luck involved. Although there are important national and world championship pairs events, all of the most prestigious titles are team games, where luck tends to balance out over sessions. Although Barry Crane was considered the best matchpoint player of all time, he was also a feared opponent in team games; virtually all of today's top players are very successful in both types of contests. So let's consider the best strategies to help you improve your results whether you are playing IMPs or matchpoints.

Experienced players have learned that the two forms of duplicate frequently require very different strategies. Because of the way each is scored, the priority in matchpoints is how often your action gains. At IMPs, the key is how much you gain (like you were playing rubber bridge).

Bob Hamman really goes to the heart of the matter with his quote. Matchpoints isn't really bridge in its purest form, because you are competing against a number of pairs and you are attempting to produce above-average results consistently. Sometimes this requires actions that would be frowned upon in a team game. Losing a board by 10 points if the field makes 2NT (120) and you make 2♠

(110) is just as devastating as if the field bids and makes a grand slam and you go down. A zero is a zero is a zero. The good news is that you can produce a top on the next board to offset the bad result.

When you are playing IMPs, you have an entirely different perspective. Your goal is safety and having the surest and the largest positive score.

You are competing with the other pairs holding your cards on each deal, so your score depends completely on the comparison with them. The key to success is HOW OFTEN you beat these other pairs, not by how much. At IMPs, the key to winning is HOW MUCH, not how often you defeat the opponents. Your results are calculated from the IMP chart and the number of IMPs you win or lose is determined by the total points after comparing the score with the other table.

At matchpoints, one overtrick can be the difference between a top and a bottom score. In a team game, the overtrick is never worth more than 1 IMP.

Let's examine some of the differences in strategy between the two forms of bridge:

1. In general, IMPs rewards solid, steady bidding and play. You rely on your teammates at the other table and they rely on you to arrive at the best contract, defeat contracts when possible, avoid errors in concentration and not to do anything crazy or silly. Matchpoints, on the other hand, usually rewards enterprising, aggressive bidding and play. Although you hope to avoid a poor score on a board, you are

trying to win every deal and every trick during that deal.

2. At IMPs, overtricks are secondary; your primary goal is to defeat the contract. At matchpoints you should fight for every trick, because it could easily be the difference between a good or bad score on this board.

3. Partscores: at IMPs, you want to ensure the SUREST positive score; at matchpoints, you strive for the MAXIMUM score and compete hard for it.

4. Doubles: As a general rule, in almost all doubling situations at IMPs, the odds favor the COWARD, not the hero. Close doubles should be avoided, especially doubling the opponents into game. It should be your hand or you should be fairly sure you can defeat the contract. At matchpoints, you can make more speculative doubles. Sometimes you have to double, hoping to produce a score higher than the value of your partscore.

5. Games: At IMPs, because of the scoring scale, it's generally best to bid games that are 40% or better to make when vulnerable (assuming you aren't doubled and don't go down more than one trick). Non-vulnerable games should be bid when they are likely to make (50% or better).

At matchpoints, you should usually bid games that are 50% or better, because it is important to try to have a positive score when possible. No one can calculate the exact percentage during an auction, so these are helpful guidelines. The key point is to be aggressive at IMPs when you are vulnerable and have to decide whether to bid one more.

6. Slams: At IMPs, safety is the key. There is no reason to bid a risky 6NT when 6 of a minor seems more certain. At matchpoints, when accurate bidding allows you to reach a slam in a minor, you should evaluate the likelihood that the rest of the field will also bid it. As with IMPs, it's usually incorrect to try for an iffy higher-scoring slam, because some or much of the field might not bid any slam. When you have a wealth of HCP and it appears the field will be in slam, that's the time at matchpoints to consider a slam that isn't as safe.

7. Sacrificing: At IMPs, you should be sure it's a good sacrifice, because they are likely to double you rather than bidding higher. That said, the odds are better to sacrifice against confidently bid slams when it is likely your teammates will reach the makeable slam, too. Avoid phantom saves (a sacrifice when the opponents wouldn't have made their contract) at all costs. At matchpoints, sacrifices against games are a far better proposition than in team games. You may earn an excellent score losing 300 against their non-vulnerable game (420) or 500 against their vulnerable game (620), so you can be aggressive.

Summary of Winning Tactics
for Both Forms of Competition

A. Concentrate as much as you can on each trick of every deal. If you are going to lose focus, probably the best time to make a careless error is when playing IMPs and the only question is whether an overtrick is made (But remember, many matches have been lost by the smallest of margins, 1 or 2 IMPs).

B. At matchpoints, strive to take every trick possible, while at IMPs, the main goal is to make or set a contract.

C. The only time you should seriously consider bidding a game that rates to be less than a 50% probability is vulnerable at IMPs.

D. At IMPs, it's important to estimate how you stand as the match progresses. Although you don't want to do anything crazy (especially when you have competent teammates at the other table), the goal is to win, whether by 1 IMP or 100 IMPs, so the state of the match can influence your actions. At matchpoints, each board is a separate competition and you are trying to maximize your result on each board (never give up and keep grinding away until the session is over).

E. At IMPs, safety plays are important, because you want to ensure making your contract. At matchpoints, they are seldom used, because overtricks are significant.

F. At both forms of bridge, be a great partner and teammate. As I have advised, make sure you play with friendly, tolerant, fun people.

$\spadesuit \ \heartsuit \ \diamondsuit \ \clubsuit$

SIXTY-ONE

Visualizing Partner's Hand Is a Crucial Part of Accurate Bidding

"Imagination is more important than knowledge."

–Albert Einstein

THE CLASSICAL APPROACH to bidding has been that you and your partner conduct a dialogue, a conversation between equals. You describe your hand to partner and he does the same for you. Eventually, in most auctions, one of you makes a bid that describes the bidder's hand and narrowly defines its strength. At this point the other player becomes the captain of the auction (Principle #42 discussed "Who is the Captain?"). It is now up to that player to suggest or decide the contract, because he knows the combined assets of the partnership. In every auction, someone must take the bull by the horns and make the decisive bid. Once your partner has given you every bit of information possible, you may still have to conjure up an image of his HCP and distribution, decide how well it will complement your hand, and judge your prospects. Forming a picture of your partner's hand from his bidding (and the opponents' bidding as well or lack thereof) is a crucial skill.

Many players think only of their own cards, but good players look further. They mentally place certain cards around the table during the auction and estimate how good the chances will be in the contract they are considering. One helpful rule of thumb is:

IF A SUITABLE MINIMUM FOR PARTNER'S BIDDING WILL MAKE A CONTRACT LAYDOWN, BID IT.

For example if you hold:

♠ A K 8 5 4 3
♥ A J 7 6
♦ K 3
♣ 3

Partner raises your 1♠ opening to 2♠. You can count your points if you want to, but a realistic approach is to bid 4♠. You are a heavy favorite in 4♠ if partner has no more than the ♥K and ♠Jxxx. In fact, if partner has not much more than xxxx xx Jxxx Qxx, you will make game when the ♦A is onside and spades are 2-1. Add the ♦Q to dummy and you make 4♠ for sure as long as spades are 2-1.

The important corollary to this rule of thumb is:

IF YOU ARE CONSIDERING A CONTRACT FOR WHICH PARTNER MUST HOLD JUST THE RIGHT CARDS, FORGET IT.

1. Your hand is:

♠ K 6 5
♥ 8
♦ A Q 8 6 4
♣ A J 5 3

Partner responds 1♥ to your 1♦ opening and rebids 2♥ over 2♣. How many hearts should partner have? How many high-card points? What call do you make?

2. Your hand is:

♠ —
♥ Q 7
♦ K J 6 5 2
♣ Q J 8 5 4 2

East opens 1♦ (with both sides vulnerable), West responds 1NT, passed around to you. What distribution should your partner have? How much high-card strength? Would you balance with 2♣?

3. Your hand is:

♠ K 5
♥ A K 7 6 3
♦ A 8 6 4
♣ A Q

East passes and you open 1♥. Partner raises you to 4♥ (preemptive). What distribution should your partner have? Can you visualize a hand for him that would make slam a good contract?

4. Your hand is:

♠ K Q 8 5
♥ A J 7 5 3
♦ A 6
♣ A J

PARTNER	YOU
1♠	3♥
4♥	5♦
6♥	?

What is partner likely to have in hearts? Assuming a grand slam is possible, in what strain do you bid it?

5. Your hand is:

♠ K 7 5
♥ J 5
♦ 8 7 6 4
♣ 9 8 6 4

West opens 1♦, partner cuebids 2♦ (strong), East bids 3♣, you pass, West raises to 4♣ , partner bids 5♣(!). What do you do at your turn?

6. Your hand is:

♠ 8 6 4
♥ A K 9 6
♦ J 5
♣ A K 4 3

SOUTH	WEST	NORTH	EAST
		Pass	1♥
Pass	1♠	2♦	2♠
?			

What do you know about partner's hand? What call do you make?

7. Your hand is:

- ♠ K
- ♥ J 3 2
- ♦ A Q 7
- ♣ A K 8 6 5 3

You open 1♣, West overcalls 1♠, partner raises to 2♣, East passes. What call do you make?

SOLUTIONS

1. Six or seven hearts and fewer than 10 HCP. Pass, before things get any worse.

2. Partner should have ten major-suit cards, since the opponents failed to find a major-suit fit. With that much distribution he would have acted over 1NT with a decent hand. West has club length since he neither responded in a major nor raised diamonds. Pass.

3. Partner probably has a singleton or void someplace, most likely in diamonds, your longest suit. As little as:

♠ Q 10 6 4
♥ J 8 6 4 3
♦ 3
♣ 8 7 6

gives you a play for slam, so you should at least try to get there. Even a direct 6♥ would be reasonable.

4. This is a famous hand. Partner must have the missing heart honors since he leaped to slam without the ♣A and your spade honors. Bid 7♥, since partner's fifth spade can provide a crucial discard for one of your minor-suit losers. Partner's hand:

♠ A J 10 9 5
♥ K Q 10 5
♦ Q 6 5
♣ 5

5. Bid 6♠. Partner committed your side to five of a major, and for all he knows, you have nothing.

6. Partner must hold excellent diamonds — what else can he have when you own this much high-card strength and the opponents opened and responded? Cue bid 3♥ or jump to game in diamonds.

7. Bid 3NT. West is far more likely to lead a low spade than to lay down the ♠A. A singleton king can be considered a stopper in this situation.

The following important concept from Mike Lawrence's "Complete Book of Hand Evaluation" will help you visualize and evaluate your hand, so you can make the best decision on how high to bid.

The Box Principle In Evaluating Your Hand During the Auction

Often during an auction, you will be asked to evaluate your hand. The BOX principle may be able to help you with that.

The BOX works on auctions where you have defined your hand. These auctions show examples of how this works.

WEST	NORTH	EAST	SOUTH
			1NT

Your opening notrump bid shows 15–17. No matter how the auction continues, your partner will assume you have 15–17 balanced points. Your hand is said to be in a box of hands that contains only 15–17 points with balanced distribution.

Pass	1♦	Pass	2NT

If you use 2NT as invitational, you announce a hand in a box that contains 11–12 balanced points with no four-card major. This box is very well defined.

Pass	1♥	Pass	2♥

Your 2♥ raise shows a hand that, with distribution, is worth 6-9 "support" points. If you have 10 high-card points, you have bad distribution and poor-quality points and are using your judgment.

WEST	NORTH	EAST	SOUTH
			1♣
Pass	1♠	Pass	2♠

2♠ shows 12–15 support points. According to your agreements, 2♠ may be bid with three spades or four spades. You may play that 2♠ promises four. Whatever your agreements, your hand is in the box of 12–15 points.

WEST	NORTH	EAST	SOUTH
Pass	1♠	Pass	Pass

Responder's pass shows a poor hand, usually in the 0-5 point range. This is a rather wide range in contrast to some of the other ranges. Whatever happens later in the bidding, opener will never play responder for more than 5 high-card points.

WEST	NORTH	EAST	SOUTH
Pass	1♥	Pass	3♥

This is a limit raise promising 10–11 support points and always four-card support. Never make a limit raise with three. Hence, responder's box can include 8–11 high-card points with allowances for distribution.

WEST	NORTH	EAST	SOUTH
			3♠

What this shows depends on your agreements. You probably have some minimum and maximum agreements that depend on the vulnerability. If not vulnerable versus vulnerable, your box might be in the range of (say) 4–9 high card points. This box of hands will change from partnership to partnership.

Some auctions do not define your hand. Auctions like the following are not well defined.

WEST	NORTH	EAST	SOUTH
1♣	1♠		

A 1♠ overcall shows from a sane 9 points up to some 17 counts. At this moment, your partner has a vague understanding of your values.

WEST	NORTH	EAST	SOUTH
Pass	1♦	Pass	1♠

A 1♠ response shows 6–20 points. This auction says almost nothing about responder's hand other than that he has four spades and does not have a hopeless hand.

WEST	NORTH	EAST	SOUTH
			1♣
Pass	1♥	Pass	1♠

Your box is from 11 high-card points which you might have if your hand contains some shape and fair suits up to an 18 high-card point hand that was not good enough for a stronger rebid.

The Important Aspect of the Box Principle

If you have boxed your hand and partner starts asking questions, you should have a fairly easy decision as to what to do. Two examples:

EXAMPLE ONE

No One Vulnerable • North Deals • You are South

♠ 8
♥ J 10 7 6 2
♦ 6 5 4 2
♣ J 10 9

WEST	NORTH	EAST	SOUTH
	1♠	Pass	Pass
2♦	Dbl	Pass	2♥
Pass	3♥	Pass	?

Your hand, initially, was not good. It's still not a good hand but it's showing signs of life. Partner's double of 2♦ should make you feel much better about things than you did a moment ago. You should be pleased to bid 2♥. Might you think of bidding more?

Your partner isn't done. He raises to 3♥, a clear question. Do you like your hand?

You may not like it but you are being asked if your hand is good *given that you have already announced a bad hand*.

Let's see. Your initial pass said you had 0–5.

When you bid 2♥, you still did not admit to having any values.

When partner raised to 3♥, his message is clearly:

"Do you have anything at all that you like?"

Given that you have a bad hand, something partner is aware of, you should evaluate in that light. By now you should appreciate just how good your hand is.

You have not four hearts, you have five. You have the J-10 of hearts, something that may come in handy.

You have a singleton spade. This has potential.

You have four diamonds. No wasted cards opposite partner's shortness in diamonds.

And you have the J-10-9 of clubs. Your partner should have some club values and your club holding will help reinforce whatever your partner has in the suit.

Bid 4♥ and expect to make an overtrick.

If, when partner bid 3♥, you fell into the unthinking trap of saying you had just two points, you have done a bad job. The Box principle helps you realize that your hand is at the top of what your partner expects.

Here's a similar hand.

♠ 8 2
♥ 8 7 6 2
♦ Q 4 2
♣ Q 5 4 3

This hand has 4 high-card points. But it's worth less than half of the hand from the hand you actually held. The queen of diamonds, for example, rates to have zero value.

EXAMPLE TWO

No One Vulnerable • North Deals • You are South

♠ Q J 4
♥ K 8 5 2
♦ 4 3
♣ 9 8 7 3

WEST	NORTH	EAST	SOUTH
	1♠	Pass	2♠
Pass	3♦	Pass	?

You showed a hand normally in the 6–9 point range. Bidding 3♠ at this point is acceptable. Your spades are nice but you have only three of them. Your king of hearts has potential. Your doubleton diamond has potential too. If you had one more spade, this would be a certain 4♠ bid. As it is, bidding 3♠ is a decent choice. Your hand is worth about 7 points and that is in the minimum range for your bidding. The auction continues with an unexpected call from partner. Normally, on this sequence, your partner passes. Instead he bids 4♥. This bid commits your side to game. Partner must be looking for a slam. What do you think now?

WEST	NORTH	EAST	SOUTH
	1♠	Pass	2♠
Pass	3♦	Pass	3♠
Pass	4♥	Pass	?

Keep this in mind. Your partner heard you turn down a game try. Your 3♠ bid showed a minimum hand for your bidding. Given you have limited your hand, the hand you have has grown. Your spades are very good. You might have had 9-7-3. Your king of hearts has been confirmed as a terrific card. Your doubleton diamond is still a possible asset.

In other words, having warned partner that you have something in the 6–7 point range, you actually have much more. All of your points are working. You can't, under the circumstances, have a better hand.

You could bid 6♠.

You could also ask for aces, just to make sure you have enough aces.

You might kick it back to your partner with a 5♠ bid.

You might cue bid the king of hearts.

The one thing that you should not do is bid 4♠. You can say NO only so many times.

What might partner have for his bidding? Here's one layout.

♠ A K 9 7 6 3   ♠ Q J 4
♥ A Q 3   ♥ K 8 5 2
♦ K Q J 8   ♦ 4 3
♣ —   ♣ 9 8 7 3

Slam is good, as South expected.

KEY

When asked to evaluate your hand, keep in mind what you have already promised. Do you have a maximum for your bidding, exactly what you have promised, or a minimum for your bidding?

Appendices

Dear Reader:

I hope you have enjoyed my effort and increased your bridge knowledge. My main goals are for you to have more fun in life and bridge, be ethical and elevate your game. If you have learned from this book, there is also volume 2 available.

I've added a few extra serious essays that include more about ethics. Then I have shared my lists of favorite movies, books, songs, basketball players and quotes. Hopefully, many of you will compile your own lists; after all, there is plenty to savor about life away from the bridge table. I'd love to hear from you whether you found my writing to be helpful and entertaining or if you wish to contribute constructive criticism.

You may email me at:

info@baronbridgetravel.com

or

goosebag@aol.com

All the best, Randy

ACBL's Zero Tolerance Policy

THE ULTIMATE PURPOSE of the ZT policy is to create a much more pleasant atmosphere in our NABCs. We are attempting to eradicate unacceptable behavior in order to make the game of bridge more enjoyable for all.

The following are examples of commendable behavior, which, while not required, will significantly contribute to the improved atmosphere:

- Being a good "host" or "guest" at the table.
- Greeting others in a friendly manner.
- Praising the bidding and/or play of the opponents.
- Having two clearly completed convention cards readily available to the opponents. (This one is a regulation, not just a nicety.)

The following are examples of behavior that will not be tolerated:

- Badgering, rudeness, insinuations, intimidation, profanity, threats or violence.
- Negative comments concerning opponents' or partner's play or bidding.
- Constant and gratuitous lessons and analyses at the table.
- Loud and disruptive arguing with a director's ruling.

If a player at the table behaves in an unacceptable manner, the director should be called immediately.

— BARBARA SEAGRAM

Courtesy of the ACBL. Reprinted from the January, 2014 Bulletin

Active Ethics

What is "Active Ethics"

The concept of "Active Ethics" rests on four pillars -

- **The Principle of Full Disclosure** — Bridge is not like Poker. Your opponents have a right to know any agreements you have whether explicit or implicit. The Alerting Regulations are a guide, and they occasionally change. But if you think a simple "alert" (or even non alert) might fool your opponent, then over-alert! When you are the declaring side, make sure any heretofore undisclosed or misdisclosed agreements are straightened out for the opponents before the opening lead. If it involves a failure to alert or misinformation, there is still an irregularity that may need to be adjudicated by a director, but at least you have mitigated the damage. If you are the defending side, unfortunately you may not clarify the situation for the opponents until the hand is over. It may well be best to call the director to adjudicate if there was potential damage.
- **Conventions** — Along with the Principle of Full Disclosure, it is important to know your agreements. How often do we sit down with a new partner and agree to play some convention and never discuss follow-up situations? It is impossible to discuss every situation, but certainly you should know the more common sequences. Not only is this Actively Ethical, it will improve your Bridge results in the long run! Of course, bad feelings are

created when you get lucky with your misunderstanding and the opponents get fixed! That is not Actively Ethical!

- **Friendly Demeanor** — Bridge is a serious game and the competition can be intense. But unlike many activities Bridge is often played with and against players of unequal ability. The Actively Ethical player is courteous, friendly, and always tries to make his opponents feel at ease. The Actively Ethical player compliments opponents on their good play and never humiliates or criticizes partner nor opponents. The Actively Ethical player calls the Director in a pleasant tone and accepts rulings with graciousness, if he does not agree and even if he wishes to appeal the ruling. The keys are respect and the Golden Rule.

- **Tempo and Pace of Play** — Bridge is a thinking game and sometimes a player needs time. But in general players should maintain a consistent tempo, neither too fast nor too slow, and pausing after "skip bids" (even though there is no longer a Stop card). Also, a player should do his utmost to play within the allotted time. When he does fall behind, it is incumbent on his partnership to catch up as quickly as possible. It is painful to follow a pair who uses 3 minutes of your 15 minute round every time, and sometimes it slows the entire field! If your Bridge experience rests on these four pillars, you will make the game more pleasant for everyone.

C-h-e-a-t-i-n-g

by Robb Gordon

Cheat (verb):
Act dishonestly or unfairly to gain an advantage,
especially in a game or examination.

In bridge, the worst kind of cheating is collusive cheating by a partnership — where partners agree to transmit information to each other by means other than normal bidding and play. This has been done through placement of cards, tapping of feet, coughing and many other means. Fortunately, this type of cheating is rare, but unfortunately it is sometimes difficult to detect.

Following closely behind are individual acts to try to gain information on a board — frequently called a "wire." This is accomplished by wandering around the playing area surreptitiously glancing at tables to see cards, deliberately listening for table talk from adjacent tables, or somehow gaining access to hand records.

Lesser infractions usually involve the use of unauthorized information, whether it is accidentally hearing information from a different table and not reporting it to the director, or taking advantage of partner's mannerisms, breaks in tempo, or incorrect explanations. Sometimes it involves concealing an infraction, such as claiming in order to cover up a revoke, or deliberately not correcting your or partner's mis-explanation when it is appropriate to do so.

Many, perhaps most of these latter infractions may be unintentional. For this reason, there are two different laws written that involve unauthorized information — Law 16, most frequently cited, is a "civil" violation in the sense that it doesn't suggest intent on the part of the infractor, rather just a choice of action that is not available under the law due to the unauthorized information.

Note here that breaking tempo is an irregularity — it is not an infraction. We all need to think sometimes. But partner is not supposed to be able to gain advantage from that.

The second law covering this issue is Law 73, which clearly states that a player may not deliberately use unauthorized information to his benefit — this is the "criminal" violation. How and when which of these laws is applied is a subject for a different article, but suffice to say, if a player decides to use unauthorized information, he is in violation of Law 73.

Avoiding a violation of Law 16 and some others can be tricky. Here are a few pointers:

1 . If you or your partner give misinformation, as the declaring side, you must call the director and disclose this at the end of the auction. If you are the defending side, you must bring the misinformation to opponents' attention at the end of the hand, giving them the opportunity to seek redress if they feel they are damaged.

2. If you receive unauthorized information from an outside source, you must call the director and inform him away from the table of the information received. Sometimes he may be able to adjust positions or take some other action which will make the board playable.

3. If you receive unauthorized information from partner by a break in tempo or otherwise, know that you must choose from among logical alternatives one not suggested by the unauthorized information. To do otherwise even if you were "always" going to take that action creates a no-win

situation for you. If unsuccessful, you keep your result. If successful, the result will be adjusted.

What to do when you observe cheating or other irregularities

One of the worst offenses in bridge is to publicly accuse another player of cheating or of being unethical. Do not ever do this! It can get you in big trouble — subject to discipline under our Code of Disciplinary Regulations, with up to 180 days probation and/or up to 180 days suspension. It can also get you sued!

If you become aware of one of the worst kinds of cheating, privately take your information to a tournament official — the Recorder or director-in-charge. That way, an investigation can be done without the accused being embarrassed, and without the accused knowing he is being investigated, which may make it easier to gather evidence. If one of the more mundane violations occurs at the table, whether you think it deliberate or not, simply call the director. Describe the irregularity, but do not try to characterize the intent of your opponent. That is for the director to investigate.

In this way, bridge "justice" will be achieved most effectively without making you the bad guy.

The Worst Opening Lead in the History of Bridge

BY LARRY COHEN

I actually witnessed this one at the table. I was South, playing with David Berkowitz in the National Championships in Hawaii in 2005.

Dealer West • N-S Vulnerable

Berkowitz
- ♠ K 3
- ♥ A K Q J 10 9 2
- ♦ 6
- ♣ A Q 3

Fantoni
- ♠ Q 6 2
- ♥ 3
- ♦ A Q 10 8 7 4 3
- ♣ 6 5

Nunes
- ♠ A J 10 9 8 5
- ♥ 7 5 4
- ♦ 9 5
- ♣ 8 2

Cohen
- ♠ 7 4
- ♥ 8 6
- ♦ K J 2
- ♣ K J 10 9 7 4

WEST	NORTH	EAST	SOUTH
3 ♦	Double	Pass	3NT
Pass	6NT	All pass	

Italian world champion, **FULVIO FANTONI,** preempted 3♦ with the West hand. David Berkowitz (too strong to overcall 4♥) doubled. With clubs stopped and the form of scoring ("matchpoint oriented") I tried 3NT. David, without checking for aces (4NT would have been invitational), jumped to 6NT off 2 aces. Embarrassing!

What would you lead as West? It is easy to see now that there were several winning solutions. The ♦A, to look at dummy, would have worked (followed by the "obvious" spade switch). Even better would be an opening spade lead. Much better. East could win and play the ♦9 through my ♦K J. West could win, continue spades, and East, after taking 6 spade tricks, could play his other diamond through. Now the defense gets 7 diamond tricks. All 13 tricks on a spade lead — down 12! But, West, after long thought, guessed to lead a heart! I had the first 13 tricks. I claimed amidst a flurry of Italian cursing — likely West asking why East didn't bid 3♠ over the double to help him on lead. On the actual heart lead, I took all 13 tricks. On a spade lead, the defense could have taken all 13 tricks. That is a 26-trick swing on opening lead the all-time record. Or, at the least, tied for the all-time record.

The next time your partner is displeased with your opening lead and tells you something like: "Partner — that was the worst lead in history"...you just tell him, "No, it wasn't."

Profound Words of the Dalai Lama Who is Obviously a Bridge Expert

"You can always judge a man's character by the way he plays cards."

–Ely Culbertson

Although the Tibetan spiritual leader and one of the most compassionate humans ever to walk the earth probably hasn't had much time for card games in his life, some of his Rules of Life are profound advice for us all. These are appropriate words for everyone to take to heart.

1. When you lose, don't lose the lesson.
2. Take responsibility for your actions.
3. Silence is sometimes the best answer.
4. Great achievements require great risk.
5. If you have a disagreement, deal only with the present situation.
6. Learn the rules so you know how to break them properly.
7. When you realize you have made a mistake, take immediate steps to correct it.
8. Judge your success by what you had to give up to obtain it.

100 Movies You Might Enjoy

As we age, most of us long for the good old days, as well as hoping and praying for reasonable health to enjoy the good new days. I'm not alone in thinking that they "don't make movies like they used to." As a movie buff, I have tried to see as many worthwhile and classic films as possible. Although "different strokes for different folks," I decided it would be fun to make a list of my favorites. I'm sure I've omitted some of the ones you think are the best. Well, there is no accounting for taste in movies, spouses or politicians. Hopefully, you'll find a few new movies to add to your enjoyment of life. My top 4 movies of all-time:

1. Harold and Maude
2. Godfather II
3. Being There
4. The Shawshank Redemption

12 Angry Men
29th Street
7 Years in Tibet
A Lion in Winter
All That Jazz
All the President's Men
Amadeus
American Beauty
American Graffiti
Anne of 1000 Days
Back to the Future
Bananas
Being There
Brazil
Bridge over the River Kwai

Butch Cassidy & the Sundance Kid
Cabaret
Camelot
Casablanca
Christmas Story
Citizen Kane
Clockwork Orange
Close Encounters of the 3rd Kind
Cool Hand Luke
Crash
Driving Miss Daisy
Easy Rider
ET
Fantastia
Fargo

Field of Dreams
Forrest Gump
Fried Green Tomatoes
Gandhi
Godfather I
Godfather II
Good Morning, Vietnam
Goodbye, Mr. Chips
Goodfellas
Grand Hotel
Groundhog Day
Guess Who's Coming to Dinner
Harold and Maude
Heaven Can Wait
Hoop Dreams
Hoosiers
It's a Wonderful Life
Jackie Brown
Justice for All
Kundun
LA Confidential
Lady & the Tramp
Lawrence of Arabia
Life is Beautiful
Local Hero
Marathon Man
National Lampoon's Animal House
Network
No Country for Old Men
Oliver
One Flew Over the Cuckoo's Nest
Ordinary People
Platoon
Prince of Tides
Priscilla, Queen of the Desert

Pulp Fiction
Raging Bull
Rain Man
Regarding Henry
Reservoir Dogs
Rocky Horror Picture Show
Same Time Next Year
Saving Private Ryan
Scarface
Schinder's List
Sideways
Stand By Me
The Big Chill
The Big Lebowski
The Deer Hunter
The Graduate
The Grapes of Wrath
The Holy Grail
The Hurt Locker
The Inlaws
The King's Speech
The Last Emperor
The Meaning of Life
The Rose
The Shawshank Redemption
The Sting
The Truman Show
The Untouchables
The Usual Suspects
The Wizard of Oz
To Kill a Mockingbird
Traffic
When They Were Kings
Woodstock
Yankee Doodle Dandy

50 Books You Might Enjoy

I have been part of a book club in Louisville for over 20 years. We have now read over 150 different titles. The following list includes my favorites. If you belong to a book club or simply want to read some of the best literature produced in recent years, here are my suggestions. If you're not sure if a particular title is for you, go to Amazon and take a look at the reviews to help you decide.

A Gentleman in Moscow, Towles
A Man Called Ove, Backman
A Walk in the Woods, Bryson
Alexander Hamilton, Chernow
Calico, Joe Grisham
City of Thieves, Benioff
Corelli's Mandolin, DeBernieres
DaVinci, Code Brown
Death of Innocents, Prejean
Destiny of the Republic, Millard
Devil in the Grove, King
Devil in the White City, Larson
Doc, Russell
Goldfinch, Tartt
Harry Potter, Rowling
In the Garden of Beasts, Larson
Into Thin Air, Kronauer
Islam, Armstrong
Joe DiMaggio, Cramer
Journey Across Tibet, Wilby
Killers of the Flower Moon, Grann
Lies My Teacher Told Me, Loewen
Lonesome Dove, McMurtry

Longitudes and Attitudes, Friedman
Lucky You, Hiaassen
Marley and Me, Grogan
Memoirs of a Geisha, Golden
Not in Your Lifetime, Summers
Peter the Great, Massey
Seabiscuit, Hillenbrand
Shadow of the Silk Road, Thubron
Shantaram, Roberts
The Boys in the Boat, Brown
The Cornbread Mafia, Higdon
The Harvard Psychedelic Club, Lattin
The Help, Stockett
The Immortal Life of Henrietta Lacks, Skloot
The Johnstown Flood, McCullough
The Life of Pi, Martel
The Nine, Toobin
The Perfect Storm, Junger
The Poisonwood Bible, Kingsolver

The Red Notice, Browder
The River of Doubt, Millard
The Sandalous Summer of Sissie LaBlanc, Despres
The Things They Carried, O'Brien
The World Without Us, Weisman
The Wright Brothers, McCullough
Tuesdays with Morrie, Alboum
Unbroken, Hillenbrand

100 Songs I Have Enjoyed

Here is a list of songs that I'd like to share with you. They were all produced in 1980 or earlier. If you're not familiar with some of them, they are available on You Tube for your pleasure. Each of them has contributed to my happiness over the years in some way (It's never easy limiting a list like this).

America	*Sister Golden Hair*	1975
Beachboys	*Sloop John B*	1966
Bette Midler	*The Rose*	1979
Bill Withers	*Ain't No Sunshine*	1971
Billy Joel	*Piano Man*	1973
Bob Dylan	*Knockin' on Heavens Door*	1973
Bob Marley	*No Woman No Cry*	1975
Bob Segar	*Against the Wind*	1980
Boston	*More Than a Feeling*	1976
Brooklyn Bridge	*The Worst That Could Happen*	1968
Cat Stevens	*Trouble*	1970
Chi Lites	*Have You Seen Her?*	1971
Chi Lites	*Oh Girl*	1972
Chicago	*If You Leave Me Now*	1976
Crosby, Stills and Nash	*Our House*	1969
Crosby, Stills and Nash	*Suite Judy Blue Eyes*	1970
Crosby, Stills and Nash	*Teach Your Children*	1969
Crystal Gayle	*Don't It Make My Brown Eyes Blue*	1977
Dan Hill	*Sometimes When We Touch*	1977
Deep Purple	*Smoke on the Water*	1972
Dire Straits	*Sultans of Swing*	1978

Don McLean	*American Pie*	1971
Elton John	*Your Song*	1970
Emmylou Harris	*One of These Days*	1976
Eric Carmen	*All by Myself*	1975
Fleetwood Mac	*Go Your Own Way*	1976
Frankie Lymon & the Teenagers	*Why Do Fools Fall in Love*	1956
Fred Parris and the Satins	*In the Still of the Night*	1956
Gene Chandler	*Duke of Earl*	1962
George Harrison	*While My Guitar Gently Weeps*	1968
Gerry and the Pacemakers	*Ferry Cross the Mersey*	1964
Gilbert O'Sullivan	*Alone Again Naturally*	1972
Gladys Knight and the Pips	*Midnight Train to Georgia*	1972
Gladys Knight and the Pips	*Neither One of Us*	1973
Gladys Knight and the Pips	*The Best Thing That Ever Happened To Me*	1974
Gloria Gayner	*I Will Survive*	1978
Hank Williams	*I'll Never Get Out of This World Alive*	1952
James Taylor	*Sweet Baby James*	1970
Janis Joplin	*Get It While You Can*	1969
Janis Joplin	*Me and Bobby McGee*	1971
Jefferson Airplane	*White Rabbit*	1967
Jimi Hendrix	*Purple Haze*	1967
Jimmy Ruffin	*What Becomes of the Broken Hearted*	1966
John Lennon	*The Ballard of John and Yoko*	1969
Judy Collins	*Someday Soon*	1969
Kansas	*Dust in the Wind*	1977
Led Zeppelin	*Stairway to Heaven*	1971
Lenny Welch	*Since I Fell for You*	1976

Leo Sayer	When I Need You	1977
Linda Ronstadt	I Will Always Love You	1975
Little Anthony	Tears on My Pillow	1958
Lovin' Spoonful	Do You Believe in Magic?	1965
Lynyrd Skynyrd	Free Bird	1973
Mamas and the Papas	I Call Your Name	1966
Marianne Faithful	As Tears Go By	1964
Marshall Tucker Band	Heard It in a Love Song	1977
Mary Hopkins	Those Were the Days	1968
Melanie	Brand New Key	1972
Melvin and the Blue Notes	If You Don't Know Me By Now	1972
Moody Blues	Nights in White Satin	1967
Moody Blues	Tuesday Afternoon	1970
Neil Young	Old Man	1972
Nitty Gritty Dirt Band	Bojangles	1970
Pink Floyd	Another Brick in the Wall (Part 2)	1979
Procol Harum	Whiter Shade of Pale	1967
Queen	Bohemian Rapsody	1977
Queen	We Will Rock You/We Are the Champions	1975
Randy and the Rainbows	Denise	1963
Randy Vanwarmer	Just When I Needed You Most	1979
Robert John	Sad Eyes	1979
Roberta Flack	The First Time Ever I Saw Your Face	1969
Sam Cooke	Bring It on Home to Me	1963
Santana	Black Magic Woman	1968
Shelley Fabrey	Johnny Angel	1962
Skeeter Davis	The End of the World	1962
Stone Poneys	(Linda Ronstadt) Different Drum	1967

The Beatles	*Here Comes the Sun*	1969
The Beatles	*The Long and Winding Road*	1970
The Byrds	*Back Pages*	1967
The Doors	*People Are Strange*	1967
The Drifters	*Under the Boardwalk*	1964
The Eagles	*Hotel California*	1977
The Earls	*Remember Then*	1962
The Hollies	*He Ain't Heavy He's My Brother*	1969
The Kinks	*You Really Got Me*	1965
The Left Banke	*Walk Away Renee*	1966
The Marcels	*Blue Moon*	1961
The Marmalade	*Reflections of My Life*	1969
The Monotones	*Who Wrote the Book of Love?*	1958
The Rays	*Silhouettes on the Shade*	1957
The Rolling Stones	*Sympathy for the Devil*	1968
The Ronettes	*Be My Baby*	1963
The Seekers	*I'll Never Find Another You*	1968
The Shirelles	*Solder Boy*	1962
The Shirelles	*Will You Still Love Me Tomorrow?*	1961
The Skyliners	*Since I Don't Have You*	1958
The Stylistics	*You Make Me Feel Brand New*	1974
The Supremes	*You Can't Hurry Love*	1966
Three Degrees	*When Will I See You Again?*	1974
Tommy Edwards	*It's All in the Game*	1958

The 32
(My Lucky Number and Birthday)
Best Basketball Players
of All-Time

Since I've written three books on basketball and been a fan for over 60 years, I'll pretend that I know a little about the game. Here is one man's opinion of the greatest ever (in alphabetical order):

Kareem Abdul-Jabbar

Charles Barkley

Elgin Baylor

Larry Bird

Kobe Bryant

Bob Cousy

Steph Curry

Wilt Chamberlain

Tim Duncan

Kevin Durant

Julius Erving

Kevin Garnett

John Havlicek

Elvin Hayes

LeBron James

Magic Johnson

Michael Jordan

Jerry Lucas

Karl Malone

Moses Malone

Pete Maravich

George Mikan

Hakeem Olajuwon

Shaquille O'Neal

Bob Pettit

David Robinson

Oscar Robertson

Bill Russell

John Stockton

Wes Unseld

Bill Walton

Jerry West

Honorable Mention:

Rick Barry

Clyde Drexler

Patrick Ewing

George Gervin

Hal Greer

Kevin McHale

Dirk Nowitzki

Dolph Schayes

Isiah Thomas (Detroit)

Lenny Wilkens

Basketball Royalty

The five best players ever to step on a court (in no particular order) ... to me there is absolutely no doubt whatsoever who should be included in the top five...How could you leave any of these all-time greats off this list?

Kareem Abdul Jabbar   Michael Jordan

Wilt Chamberlain   Bill Russell

LeBron James

50 Favorite Quotes

"A man who has to go to the village to get the news hasn't heard from himself in a long time." —Thoreau

"A teacher affects eternity; he can never tell where his influence stops." —Henry Adams

"Ah, but I was so much older then, I'm younger than that now."
—The Byrds

"An eye for an eye leaves the whole world blind."
—Gandhi

"Angels can fly because they take themselves lightly."
—G.K. Chesterton

"Dignity comes not from possessing honors, but in the knowledge that we deserve them." —Aristotle

"Everything is miraculous. It is a miracle that one doesn't melt in one's bath."—Pablo Picasso

"Get busy livin' or get busy dyin'"
—Andy Dufrense, *Shawshank Redemption*

"He spoke through tears of fifteen years how his dog and him traveled about...The dog up and died and after twenty years he still grieves." —Mr. Bojangles

"I do benefits for all religions. I'd hate to blow the hereafter on a technicality." —Bob Hope

"I have noticed that nothing I never said ever did me any harm."
—Calvin Coolidge

"I know not what weapons World War III will be fought with, but World War IV will be fought with sticks and stones."
—Albert Einstein

"I used to believe in reincarnation, but that was in a past life."
—Paul Krassner

"In the cherry blossom's shade, there's no such thing as a stranger." —Issa

"It is by spending oneself that one becomes rich." —Sarah Bernhardt

"It takes a long time to understand nothing."—Edward Dahlberg

"Life is like stepping onto a boat that is about to sail out to sea and sink." —Shunryu Suzuki

"Never think that war, no matter how necessary, nor how justified, is not a crime." —Ernest Hemingway

"No matter how cynical you get, it is impossible to keep up."
—Jane Wagner

"No one cares how much you know until they know how much you care." —Theodore Roosevelt

"Oh, if you're a bird, be an early bird and catch the worm for your breakfast plate. If you're a bird, be an early bird, but if you're a worm, sleep late." —Shel Silverstein

"People are more than the worst thing they have ever done in their life." —Sister Helen Prejean

"Play for more than you can afford to lose and you will learn the game." —Winston Churchill

"Real learning comes when the competitive spirit has ceased."
—Jiddu Krishnamurti

"Seek the wisdom of the ages, but look at the world through the eyes of a child." —Ron Wild

"Sometimes there just aren't enough rocks." —Forrest Gump

"Spend the afternoon; you can't take it with you." —Anne Dillard

"The best mind-altering drug is truth." —Lily Tomlin

"The fish in the water that is thirsty needs serious professional counseling." —Kabir

"The frog does not drink up the pond in which he lives." —Native American

"The kings and dictators and the mighty of the world accomplish their works with great noise, with speeches and drums and loud-speakers and brass and the thunder of bombers. But God works in silence." —Thomas Merton

"The Messiah will come only when he is no longer necessary." —Frank Kafka

"The most important question for a person to answer is whether the universe is a friendly or unfriendly place." —Albert Einstein

"The only thing necessary for the triumph of evil is for good people to do nothing." —Edmund Burke

"The point of life is not to succeed; the point of life is to die trying." —Edna St. Vincent Millay

"The stupid neither forgive or forget; the naïve forgive and forget; the wise forgive but do not forget." —Thomas Szasz

"The thing I remember most about successful people I've met through the years is their obvious delight in what they're doing." —Fred Rogers

"There are ways but the Way is uncharted." —Taoist

"There is but one success, to be able to spend your life in your own way. May each of us have this success." —Christopher Morley

"There is never a better measure of what a person is than what he does when he's absolutely free to choose." —William M. Bulger

"There is no limit to the good a man can do if he doesn't care who gets the credit." —Robert L. Bernstein

"Trouble, oh trouble move away, I have seen your face and it's too much for me today." —Cat Stevens

"Trust in God, but tie up your camel." —Arab proverb

"Truth is something you stumble into when you think you are going someplace else." —Jerry Garcia

"We are all condemned on Death Row; we just don't know the method of execution." —Victor Hugo

"We dance round in a ring and suppose, but the Secret sits in the middle and knows." —Robert Frost

"What is a weed? A plant whose virtues have not yet been discovered." —Ralph Waldo Emerson

"When I die, I want to go peacefully and quietly in my sleep like my grandfather did, not screaming and shouting like the passengers in his car at the time." —Robert Fulghum

"You can count how many seeds are in the apple, but not how many apples are in the seed." —Ken Kersey

"You can't stop the waves, but you can learn to surf."
—Jack Kornfield

I enjoy visiting bridge clubs. If you manage a club
and would like to have me lecture there
and bring some of my books, please contact me.

RANDY BARON

info@baronbridgetravel.com
or goosebag@aol.com

502-558-0627
